Environmental Philosophy

D0062410

Environmental Philosophy

From Theory to Practice

Sahotra Sarkar

A John Wiley & Sons, Inc., Publication

This edition first published 2012
© 2012 John Wiley & Sons, Inc.

Wiley-Blackwell is an imprint of John Wiley & Sons, formed by the merger of Wiley's global
Scientific, Technical and Medical business with Blackwell Publishing.

Registered Office
John Wiley & Sons Ltd, The Atrium, Southern Gate, Chichester, West Sussex, PO19 8SQ,
United Kingdom

Editorial Offices
350 Main Street, Malden, MA 02148-5020, USA
9600 Garsington Road, Oxford, OX4 2DQ, UK
The Atrium, Southern Gate, Chichester, West Sussex, PO19 8SQ, UK

For details of our global editorial offices, for customer services, and for information about
how to apply for permission to reuse the copyright material in this book please see our
website at www.wiley.com/wiley-blackwell.

The right of Sahotra Sarkar to be identified as the author of Environmental Philosophy:
From Theory to Practice has been asserted in accordance with the UK Copyright, Designs
and Patents Act 1988.

Library of Congress Cataloging-in-Publication Data

Sarkar, Sahotra.
  Environmental philosophy : from theory to practice / Sahotra Sarkar.
    p. cm.
  Includes bibliographical references and index.
  ISBN 978-0-470-67181-8 (hardcover : alk. paper) – ISBN 978-0-470-67182-5 (pbk. : alk. paper)
  1. Environmental sciences–Philosophy. 2. Environmental ethics. 3. Environmentalism. I. Title.
  GE40.S28 2012
  333.72–dc23   2011022688

A catalogue record for this book is available from the British Library.

This book is published in the following electronic formats: ePDFs 9781118121399; ePub 9781118121405;
mobi 9781118121412

Set in 10.5/13.5pt Palatino by Thomson Digital, Noida, India
Printed in Malaysia by Ho Printing (M) Sdn Bhd

1 2012

To Katherine

Contents

Acknowledgments

My first debt is to the many students and post-doctoral researchers at the University of Texas at Austin and the Universidad Nacional Autónoma de México who have explored the issues treated in this book with me for the last decade. Listed in alphabetical order, Anshu Aggarwal, Francisco Botello, Rowena Cerro, Michael Ciarleglio, David Frank, Trevon Fuller, Justin Garson, Patricia Illoldi-Rangel, Heather Keil, Chris Kelley, Miguel Linaje, Maria Cecilia Londoño, Vanessa Lujan, Kelly McConnell, Alexander Moffett, Mariana Montoya, Ian Nyberg, Chris Pappas, Baris Parkan, Samraat Pawar, Chissa-Louise Rivaldi, Nancy Shackelford, Neil Sinhababu, Blake Sissel, and Ophelia Wang all deserve special mention.

Over the last fifteen years, a large number of colleagues and collaborators from around the world have similarly contributed to the development of these ideas. I may have inadvertently left out some (for which, following accepted convention, I apologize in advance) but the list must include (again listed in alphabetical order) J. Baird Callicott, Kelley Crews, Kevin de Laplante, James S. Dyer, Larry Gilbert, Ramachandra Guha, Dale Jamieson, Lynn Maguire, Chris Margules, Katie McShane, Bryan Norton, Jay Odenbaugh, Anya Plutynski, Víctor Sánchez-Cordero, Bill Wimsatt, and Ken Young. Thanks are also due to all members of the Complex Environmental Decisions Working Group at the (United States) National Center for Ecological Analysis and Synthesis at the University of California—Santa Barbara (2007–2008), who contributed much to my understanding of many of the issues discussed here.

Acknowledgments

For critical comments on the entire manuscript, thanks are due to Katie McShane and three helpful anonymous reviewers for Wiley-Blackwell. For comments on individual chapters, thanks are due to David Frank and Justin Garson. The material on which this book is based was presented to audiences at Iowa State University, the Middle East Technical University (Turkey), St. Michael's College, St. Norbert's College, Universidad Autónoma del Estado de Morelos, Universidad Nacional Autónoma de México, the University of Idaho, the University of Queensland, the University of Texas, the University of Utah, Washington State University, the Ashoka Trust for Research in Ecology and the Environment (India), the Congreso Nacional de Mastozoología (México), Conservation International (Indonesia; Washington, DC), the International Centre for Integrated Mountain Development (Nepal), the International Forum on Climate Change and Biodiversity (UNESCO; Republic of Korea), Pronatura (México), the Society for Conservation Biology, and the World Wildlife Fund (Canada). Many members of those audiences provided comments that were food for further reflection.

Needless to say, none of the individuals mentioned here should *ipso facto* be regarded as agreeing with the views expressed in this book. Some have been harsh critics, and I have benefited from that criticism. Similarly, errors and infelicities remain my sole responsibility. Finally, this work was supported by the United States NSF Grant No. SES-0645884, 2007–2010.

List of Acronyms

AOGCM	Atmosphere Ocean General Circulation Model
CI	Conservation International
EKVE	Ecomuseum Kristianstads Vattenrike
EMIC	Earth-system Model of Intermediate Complexity
ESA	[United States] Endangered Species Act
GBIF	Global Biodiversity Information Facility
GCM	General Circulation Model
GM	Genetically modified
ICIMOD	International Centre for Integrated Mountain Development
IPCC	Intergovernmental Panel on Climate Change
IUCN	World Conservation Union (formerly known as the International Union for the Conservation of Nature and Natural Resources)
KV	Kristianstads Vattenrike
LULC	Land Use and Land Cover
MOSOP	Movement for the Survival of the Ogoni People
NGO	Non-governmental organization
PCB	Polychlorinated biphenyl
PP	Precautionary Principle
PVA	Population viability analysis
RCM	Regional climate model
SER	Society for Ecological Restoration
UCC-CRJ	United Church of Christ's Commission for Racial Justice
UN	United Nations

List of Acronyms

UNESCO   United Nations Educational, Scientific and
             Cultural Organization
US   United States
USAID   United States Agency for International Development
WCED   United Nations World Commission on Environment
             and Development
WTP   Willingness to pay
WWF   WorldWide Fund for Nature (in Canada and
             the United States, World Wildlife Fund)

1

Introduction

The natural world seems to be deteriorating around us largely as a result of our actions. Urban sprawl spreading along the highways of Texas (and elsewhere throughout the North; that is, the "developed" world) has made it harder and harder for us to get to a spot where we can enjoy nature not dominated by human artefacts. Increasing numbers of people driving along these highways are polluting the atmosphere, besides accelerating climate change. Texas is slowly but surely running dry, with less and less water reaching the ocean along its rivers: the current water use patterns cannot be sustained for more than a generation.[1] In central Texas, two bird species, the Golden-cheeked Warbler (*Dendroica chrysoparia*) and the Black-capped Vireo (*Vireo atricapilla*), are legally designated as endangered (as defined by the United States Endangered Species Act (ESA)) because of loss of their breeding habitat to residential, industrial, and commercial development. A rapidly spreading invasive species, the imported red fire ant (*Solenopsis invicta*), which thrives on fragmented habitats (a result of human land use choices), is threatening many native species with extinction. For the same reason, Ashe juniper (*Juniperus ashei*) is aggressively spreading over the landscape, replacing much of the original plant communities. Tallgrass prairie, which originally covered a large part of the region, has almost entirely disappeared, typically replaced by monocultures of planted crops. In southeastern Texas, it has cost millions of dollars to rescue the Whooping Crane (*Grus americana*), the population of which had declined to perhaps 15

Environmental Philosophy: From Theory to Practice, First Edition. Sahotra Sarkar.
© 2012 John Wiley & Sons Inc. Published 2012 by John Wiley & Sons Inc.

individuals in the late 1930s. In Texas, as elsewhere, cattle, poultry, and other animals are being bred to be killed and consumed, sometimes in appalling conditions in order to keep prices low. These are genuine environmental problems.

There are other problems that may or may not be about the environment (part of the project of environmental philosophy is to help determine whether these problems are *environmental* problems). Since the 1990s, the Sierra Club in the United States has periodically been torn apart by a minority of members trying to get it to adopt an official stance against immigration into the United States.[2] According to this minority, these immigrants would increase the population of the United States and exacerbate already critical environmental problems. Moreover, they claim, immigrants from poorer countries such as México would adopt over-consumptive Northern lifestyles and would thus consume much more of Earth's resources than they would if they remained mired in poverty at home. Whether members of this minority are genuinely motivated by concern for the environment, or whether they are simply paranoid nativists and racists hiding behind the banner of environmentalism, remains a hotly contested issue. There is much to argue over, for instance, whether immigrants from countries such as México would really end up having over-consumptive lifestyles (like those of many white US self-described environmentalists with their oil-guzzling sports utility vehicles) and whether, even if the immigrants were to opt for over-consumption, their descendants, because of cultural changes in their new home, would have sufficiently lower birth rates to vitiate any possible effect of over-consumption. However, there is little reason to doubt that over-consumption of resources is a problem and that it depends both on lifestyle choices and population sizes.

What Is Environmental Philosophy?

Few would deny that environmental problems must be faced, and that solving these problems is essential for humanity to continue to flourish on Earth. But what has philosophy got to do with this? The answer is: a lot, and much more than you would initially expect. How do we distinguish between a genuine environmental problem and one that is not? It depends on how we define what the environment is and that, as we shall see, is a non-trivial philosophical problem (Chapter 2). Defining many other concepts used to discuss environmental issues is equally problematic: these include biodiversity (Chapter 5), ecological integrity (Chapter 6), and sustainability (Chapter 7). *Conceptual analysis*, as practiced within philosophy, is critical to their clarification. Without clarity and precision we may well make unwise decisions. For instance, if we define biodiversity incorrectly, we may end up wasting resources on biota that do not merit attention while ignoring those that do.

Moreover, should we be concerned only with the flourishing of humanity in the future? Or should we include other species? Ecosystems? What about mountains and rivers? When we choose what to eat or wear, should we worry about the harm to other species? Does it matter whether individuals of those species that we consume have the capacity to feel pain? How do we even know when an animal feels pain? Do we have responsibilities to future generations that will be affected by climate change? Within academic philosophy, environmental ethics has traditionally debated these issues (Chapter 3). The relevant questions are not purely academic. They affect how we frame policy—from what parts of nature we conserve to how we experiment with animals.

Who should be held to blame for our environmental problems? Only the proximate "offenders"; for instance, poor pastoralists in east Africa "encroaching" on a national park to gather fodder? Or should we follow the chain of explanation much further, wondering how such poverty came to be institutionalized in the first place? Is colonialism to blame? Are Northern descendants of colonialists responsible? Environmental philosophy also embraces questions such as these, which lie at the foundation of what is now often called "political ecology" (Chapter 8). Social and political philosophy have much to contribute to these issues.

Scientific questions about the environment are mostly studied within the field of ecology. How are the results of this science to be integrated with the values that frame what we think we should do with the environment? Once again, this is a philosophical problem (Chapter 4). Ecology is rarely good at predicting the future, especially for large, complex systems such as entire continent-sized landscapes. Yet, the uncertain results *must* be used to inform practical environmental policy. We need to know the quantitative effects of carbon emissions on global warming to set goals for carbon trading regimes. We need to know how reduced water flow will affect downstream fisheries before we approve damming a river. In typical cases, we do not have time to wait before making a decision. Taking time to gather more data is not an option. We almost never have time—or resources—to survey all species in a region before deciding what parts (if any) should be protected. Moreover, many environmental decisions are irreversible. Many ecosystems, once destroyed, may never regenerate. Given all these constraints, can decisions ever be rational? What does it mean to be rational in this context?

Environmental philosophy also studies the sorts of questions broached in the last paragraph, many of which belong to epistemology (the theory of knowledge) and the philosophy of science, and others to decision theory. It should be clear that environmental philosophy is a highly applied discipline, intimately engaged with the world, and may well have much to contribute to the solution of environmental problems.

What's Special about Environmental Philosophy?

First, environmental ethics attempts to enlarge the domain of traditional (that is, human) ethics by extending our moral concern to non-human entities, to individual animals and plants, to entire non-human species, and sometimes even to inanimate objects. We will examine these issues in Chapter 3. Second, as noted earlier, worrying about the effects of the uncertainty of ecological predictions is part of epistemology and the philosophy of science. But the extent of the uncertainty takes us into new conceptual territory, especially when it must be addressed in practical decision contexts. We discuss decision theory and other philosophical issues at the foundations of the environmental sciences in Chapter 4. Third, environmental philosophy embraces interdisciplinarity to an extent that is not matched by any other part of philosophy, not even by the philosophy of science (which is necessarily interdisciplinary because of its contact with the sciences). The environmental sciences, as we shall see in several chapters of this book (especially Chapter 5, Chapter 6, and Chapter 7), are highly interdisciplinary. Environmental philosophy must not only accommodate all this interdisciplinarity but also add to them normative concerns from epistemology, ethics, and aesthetics.

The academic environmental disciplines, such as conservation biology and restoration ecology, are explicitly goal-oriented. For instance, the aim of conservation biology is to maintain biodiversity, the aims of restoration ecology are to achieve historical fidelity and ecological integrity, and a variety of resource management sciences aim to ensure sustainability. As we shall see in Chapter 5, Chapter 6, and Chapter 7, each of these goals—diversity, fidelity, integrity, and sustainability—is imbued with cultural norms. Now discussion of norms—indeed, of *normativity* in general—is inherently philosophical in the sense that philosophical arguments play the role of adjudicating between the values expressed by the norms. They help identify which values and norms we should embrace and to what extent. The task is not simple: goals may be incompatible. For instance, biodiversity and historical fidelity may be incompatible if a rare and vulnerable species has recently moved into a new habitat. In cases such as these, environmental philosophy is special because what is decided within it is so intimately related to the pursuit of the environmental sciences. Moreover, these sciences are equally intimately connected to practical policy. Environmental philosophy may make a difference to what happens in practice.

Finally, environmental problems raise important issues of equity and justice. Those who benefit most from the unbridled consumption of fossil fuels largely live in the North or in the affluent sections of the South (the poorer countries). (For brevity of exposition, "the North" will from now on be used in this book to include the affluent of the South.) Northern consumption of fossil fuels is a major cause of global climate change. Yet the brunt of the negative effects of climate change will be borne by the South. What does justice demand in this context? Does it require a massive transfer of resources from the North to the South? Moreover, denizens of the South may not share the values of the North; for instance, the protection of charismatic species, especially if such protection must come with the loss or diminution of already precarious livelihoods. Which values are more important? These are also issues in environmental philosophy, as will be discussed in Chapter 8, though they are equally issues in social and political philosophy without any specific concern for the environment.

Why Is Environmental Philosophy Important?

Philosophy has two important functions in almost all applied contexts:

(1) It helps clarify what we do: what we perceive as problems, what we set as goals, how we set those goals, and how and why we choose strategies to achieve those goals. For instance, when we argue that a habitat patch should be set aside for nature, are we doing so because of a concern for the species on it, independent of perceived human interests, or because it provides beautiful scenery that we appreciate? When we think about its protection, do we mean we want no human access, less human access, or even restoration of nature at that place? Suppose our focus is on the biota. Does protection mean we want the species to persist or do we care about the welfare of each individual? And why? When we think of strategy, do we want higher ticket prices, community ownership, state intervention, or some combination of all of these? And why?

(2) Philosophy helps put things in context. Environmental problems may be connected to socio-political problems. For in-

stance, deforestation may be a result of poverty. Moreover, many of the values we cherish (in nature as well as elsewhere) may be in conflict. (Box 1.1 discusses the wildlife conservation policies that were adopted in east Africa in the late 1980s, and what philosophy could have contributed to the process.)

Box 1.1   Preserving Wildlife: Wildlife Wars in East Africa in the 1980s[3]

The 1980s saw serious declines in east Africa's elephant populations even as black rhinoceros populations were on the brink of extinction. Concern for the survival of these species—and about other wildlife declines—prompted several international non-governmental organizations (NGOs) to make African wildlife conservation a major priority. Several African governments responded to this pressure by militarizing the enforcement of wildlife laws, in particular access to national parks. Northern NGOs and the media viewed these developments as a "war" for wildlife. In 1985 Zimbabwe began the paramilitary "Operation Stronghold" commanded by former Rhodesian Defense Force officers with a mandate to track down and kill black "poachers." In 1988 Kenyan President Daniel Arap Moi issued a shoot-on-sight order to thousands of police sent into those national parks that were believed to be suffering the highest elephant losses. These losses were supposed to be due to the activities of foreign "poachers" from Somalia. In 1989, Tanzania launched "Operation Uhai" to remove "poachers," using a military strike force (of army, police, and Wildlife Division personnel). Military equipment flowing into the region included automatic assault rifles, helicopters, and remote-controlled surveillance aircraft. Virtually all funding came from the North. The British Parliament debated sending British troops to Kenya, Mozambique, and Tanzania to help protect elephants. Millions of dollars came from the United States.

While the official policy of the World Wildlife Fund (WWF) at this time was not to provide funds for guns or ammunition, in practice it disbursed such funds in Tanzania in 1987 and funded the purchase of helicopters in Zimbabwe.

Shoot-on-sight orders to kill "poachers" and "bandits" were issued in the Central African Republic, Kenya, Malawi, Tanzania, and Zimbabwe. In the Central American Republic, Bruce Hayes, a co-founder of Earth First! in the United States, hired mercenaries to shoot at "poachers," again supposedly from Somalia. These mercenaries were also given shoot-on-sight authority. Almost all these African countries declared a "war" on "poachers." More than a hundred people were killed in each of Kenya and Zimbabwe. More than three hundred were killed in Malawi and an even larger number disappeared. Park rangers in Malawi were routinely accused of systematic rape. Between 20 and 50 people were killed in Tanzania, and between 20 and 96 in Botswana. Not one of those who were killed received a trial. Human rights activists have pointed out that many victims were reported by credible witnesses to have been unarmed and that many were local residents, some of whom had been evicted to create the national parks.

What would philosophy have contributed to this situation? The issue that immediately sticks out is whether there is any moral justification in killing humans to protect animals. But there is a deeper worry: should wildlife conservation ever be conceptualized as a "war"? As Roderick Neumann puts it: "how is the protection of biodiversity by means of militarized defense of wild animals made the moral equivalent of war? Stated differently, how can what are essentially battle orders—blanket shoot-to-kill/shoot-on-sight orders—be morally justified for the case of people found illegally inside protected areas?"[4] Should concern for the environment ever lead to an endorsement of violence? Could this so-called war only have been declared because the enemy targeted to be shot at were black Africans? (Imagine declaring a war with a shoot-to-kill policy against the white ranchers who protested conservation measures for the endangered Golden-cheeked Warbler, sometimes violently, in central Texas in the 1990s.[5]) Is it that we are back to the colonial era, when black Africans were treated by the North as if they had a moral status no better than that of animals?

It does not even require a professional philosopher to note moral problems with extra-judicial killings without any trial— let alone a fair one. Given the evidence, it similarly takes little effort to be skeptical about whether those labeled as "poachers" were accurately so labeled. (The absence of fair trials for those killed prevents any confidence on this point.) Probing more deeply, there is room to worry that individuals and organizations from the North were imposing their values (wildlife preservation) on people from the South who may not share those values or may have different views about how wildlife should be preserved. In the 1980s, especially among Northern governments, transnational bodies, and NGOs, decisions about protecting nature were being made with no respect for any canon of distributive justice: there was no concern for the negative impact that national parks and wildlife conservation had on local livelihoods.

Philosophy is also important because it encourages questioning of things that are often not questioned: philosophers are often (perhaps justly) parodied for their apparently irritating habit of making obvious claims seem problematic. Many environmental problems are presented by both self-proclaimed environmentalists and the media in such a way as to generate alarm—a type of inchoate apprehension that does not encourage careful deliberation when attitudes are formed and policies are framed (for an example, see Box 1.2). Philosophy attempts to reverse this practice by treating all such claims with caution and skepticism before accepting them. For instance, the philosopher Elliott Sober once questioned, to the horror of many environmentalists, whether an individual with a starving family has any ethical responsibility not to hunt the last members of a critically endangered animal species.[9] The question was worth asking. Environmental philosophers continue to disagree about the answer.

Box 1.2 The Global 2000 Report to the President (of the United States)[6]

In 1980 the Council on Environmental Quality and the United States Department of State produced a report for President Jimmy Carter that was supposed to provide a basis for long-term planning. It appears to be a meticulous piece of scholarship based on endless graphs and computer simulations of future scenarios performed by more than 100 experts around the world over a period of three years. Its coverage was encyclopedic, including issues related to population, economic development, income, food, land, water, soil, forests, minerals, air and water pollution, species extinction, and energy.

In retrospect what is perhaps most striking is what the report had to say about species extinctions. It suggested that "between half a million and 2 million species—15 to 20 percent of all species on earth—could be extinguished by 2000, mainly because of the loss of wild habitat but also in part because of pollution."[7] This estimate was produced by Thomas Lovejoy of the WWF. The estimation process used projections of deforestation made by project experts. A variety of curves were drawn to represent the possible relationship between deforestation and extinction. These curves were not supposed to represent different scenarios; rather they were supposed to reflect the uncertainty about this relationship. Ultimately, the numbers reported came from assuming a linear relationship and by setting the expected species loss, if all forests were destroyed, at 95 percent.

Post-2000, these estimates are known to be absurdly high, a result of reveling in the doomsday scenarios that had become standard fare among environmentalists ever since the Club of Rome began to produce them in the 1970s.[8] Would philosophy have helped? Well, any philosopher of science should have pointed out that the projections had virtually no factual basis. For instance, if Lovejoy and the other "experts" had used the species-area curves customarily used by ecologists to model the relationship between the number of species and the area of forested land left, they would have come up with much lower extinction estimates. Most philosophers would have warned that policy should never be based on estimates that are so poorly rooted in facts. Ultimately, it did not matter because Ronald Reagan defeated Jimmy Carter in the 1980 United States presidential election and uniformly ignored all concerns of environmentalists.

It is not at all being suggested that the issues discussed above cannot be handled outside environmental philosophy. Given how little philosophical attention has been given to the environment (and the extent to which that attention has been narrowly restricted to environmental ethics), many of these questions have typically been most carefully explored in other contexts. What environmental philosophy does is to provide a forum for the systematic exploration of these questions, including their complicated relationships with each other.

Notes

1. See Sansom (2008). Much of the Texas analysis is based on fieldwork (Sarkar, unpublished data).
2. Clarke (2001) reviews the dispute; see also Sarkar (2005), Chapter 1.

3. This case study is from Neumann (2004); see Dowie (2009) for many other such examples.
4. Neumann (2004).
5. Welch (1994); Mann and Plummer (1995).
6. See Council on Environmental Quality and US Department of State (1981) for the full report.
7. Council on Environmental Quality and US Department of State (1981), p. 37.
8. See Meadows *et al.* (1972).
9. See Sober (1986), who distinguishes between environmental aesthetics and environmental ethics to explain the divergence of positions.

2

What Is the *Environment*?

We will begin with an issue that initially appears to be—but appearances are deceptive—a digression, the nature–nurture dispute, which has been part of Western philosophy since antiquity. Consider your musical ability (or inability, if you are like me). Those who side with nature in the traditional dispute will view it to be a result of your internal constitution, your biology. Some will further reduce it to your biological inheritance; in the twentieth century they would have attributed it to your genes. Conversely, those who opt for nurture will suggest that your ability is due to your education or exposure to music, perhaps early in life—in other words, to your environment. Nature stands contrasted to the environment. In the use of the term in the nature–nurture dispute, the nature of something is broadly what Aristotle would have called that thing's essence.

This is not how environmentalists think of nature or the environment. The problem here is with both words, *nature* and *environment*. The literary critic and theorist, Ray Williams, has persuasively argued that *nature* had already begun to take the meaning with which we will use it in this book during the medieval era.[1] The term *environment* as used by self-styled environmentalists only seems to have emerged in the latter half of the twentieth century. According to the *Oxford English Dictionary*, the term *environmentalism* when it means "concern with the preservation of the environment" only dates back to 1972, beginning in the United States, and *environmen-*

Environmental Philosophy: From Theory to Practice, First Edition. Sahotra Sarkar.
© 2012 John Wiley & Sons Inc. Published 2012 by John Wiley & Sons Inc.

talist, used in this way, is of slightly older vintage. But the concerns that we call *environmental* today have a much longer continuous history, going back several centuries in many countries. Even in the United States, the first edition of Ray Dasmann's pioneering textbook, *Environmental Conservation*, appeared in 1959 and Dasmann clearly saw his book as a contribution to an existing academic discipline that included, among other things, forestry and other resource management.[2]

It is also debatable whether *environment* (in the environmentalists' sense) has a good counterpart in almost any non-Indo-European language.[3] Roughly, it seems to be a substitute for what was called nature and was tacitly assumed to consist of features of the world not created by human action (that is, by culture). Environmental conservation may well be just a fancy new term for the old and mundane program of nature protection. But what is *nature*? In particular, are humans part of nature? In the European context, according to Williams, the separation of humans from what would be called *nature* came late, only in eighteenth-century Europe. As we shall see, the relation between nature and culture is even more complicated.

What Is Nature?

If the nature of something is its essence, then there are as many natures as there are things. Thanks to the continuing influence of Aristotle, this is how nature was typically conceptualized in medieval Europe. In Aristotle's view, each feature of the world, such as each animal or plant species, each element, and so on, had its own nature to be separately analyzed and understood. The birth of modern science in seventeenth-century Europe was a many-faceted break with that medieval heritage. One of these breaks was with the assumption that there was a single nature, rather than many natures, to be understood. Indeed, this assumption lies behind the unificatory metaphysics under which much of modern science has operated. Newton's theory of gravitation assumed that there was a single underlying force that could explain celestial and terrestrial mechanics: what makes an apple fall to the ground (in the much-retold apocryphal tale) also makes planets go around the Sun in their elliptical orbits. The eighteenth and nineteenth centuries saw chemistry brought under the aegis of universal physics. Arguably, at least, the advent of molecular biology in the twentieth century has finally shown that biology can also be integrated into the same framework.[4]

Many philosophers have interpreted these developments as a triumph of *reductionism*. Astronomy was reduced to physics; that is, the laws of physics could explain all the facts of astronomy. Subsequently, chemistry was reduced to physics; and, finally, biology is being reduced to chemistry. Physics was what was supposed to describe fundamental nature. Other philosophers have quibbled over whether these developments should be called *reductionism* on a variety of grounds. For instance, the apparently single biological phenomenon (a *type*) of the transport of molecules through cell membranes can be brought about through a variety of physical mechanisms (*tokens* in philosophical terminology). For some philosophers, reductionism requires that types be explained by (or be reduced to) types: from this perspective the chemical explanation of biological phenomena cannot be interpreted as a triumph of reductionism. Many proponents of the reductionist thesis counter by arguing that metaphysical issues, such as that of whether types are connected to types, are irrelevant to reductionism: all that matters is the epistemological question, whether the facts of one scientific field are explained by those of another.

Yet, another group of philosophers (including many who write on environmental issues) have argued that reductionism has been an unfortunate development.[5] For some, this is because reductionism has led to an anemic conception of scientific progress. For others, it is because it asserts the primacy of physical processes rather than organic ones, thereby allegedly denigrating nature. The trouble with such positions is that they seem to entail a rejection of modern science (whether or not it is interpreted as reductionist) and all its attendant benefits, including insights from the ecological sciences and medi-

15

cine. The question of reductionism deserves, and often has received, book-length treatment on its own.[6]

According to Williams, the unified conception of nature that we have inherited from the scientific revolution of the seventeenth century is supposed to have its origin in the unified conception of deity/god (that is, monotheism) that emerged in medieval Europe. For many of the natural philosophers (as scientists were called before the nineteenth century), knowing nature was a way of knowing the deity/god. What is perhaps more important is that humans were perceived as part of this nature. Nevertheless, by the eighteenth century a radical change was under way.

Williams suggests that this radical shift began with the separation of the deity/god from nature insofar as the shift made it possible to study and understand nature without worrying about the deity/god. This separation was already under way in the seventeenth century. The next step was to separate humanity from nature. According to Williams, as early as the seventeenth century, philosophers such as Thomas Hobbes were making a distinction between brute nature and what humans can achieve through improvement.[7] The Industrial Revolution in eighteenth-century Europe showed the extent to which humans could "improve" nature, which largely meant that they could transform the rest of the world to satisfy human desires. Moreover, from the separation of the deity/god from nature, the separation of humans from nature was a natural step, especially if it is assumed that humans were made in the deity's image. This separation was critical: it laid the foundation for the dichotomy between humans and nature that we often assume today.[8] But the move also had persistent critics; for instance, Rousseau and the so-called Romantics. There will be more discussion of the presumed dichotomy between nature and human culture in the next section.

In the nineteenth century, with the theory of evolution, humanity's position in the order of things came under unprecedented challenge. Far from being made in the deity's image, *Homo sapiens* had evolved from "lower" forms of life and shared a recent common ancestor with apes. The most important founder of evolutionary biology,

Charles Darwin, was willing to posit continuity between human mental capacities and animal instinct, between human culture and animal behavior.[9] Darwin was also sure that human intellectual and cultural behaviors were a product of natural selection, a result of higher reproduction rates because of those behaviors. Not all other evolutionary biologists were as convinced of the power of natural selection, but few doubted the material evolutionary origin of humanity and its complex behavioral patterns.[10] Humanity was back within nature, but the nature of nature continued to be contested. For some, nature was red in tooth and claw: from this perspective, it was an easy step to Social Darwinism, eugenics, and other atrocities perpetrated in the name of biology. For others, nature was an extraordinary interlocking system of mutual advantage: dreams of communal bliss were supposed to be based on the order of things.

Nature and Culture

Beavers build dams; humans build suburbs. Is there a salient difference? If so, what is it? Why do we call one "natural" and the other "artificial," as if it is non-natural? Moreover, as we noted earlier, both *Homo sapiens* and *Castor canadiensis* (the north American beaver) are products of evolution and it is easy enough to see how their home-building practices could have evolved through natural selection over generations. This may make us wonder whether there is a salient difference between human behavior and that of any other species. But, if there is no such difference, given that humans are part of nature, what does concern for nature (or concern for the environment) mean? By taking care of ourselves, we would be taking care of nature. If we want bigger cars, we do no harm to nature by satisfying that desire. At best, there may be prudential reasons for us not to satisfy every immediate appetite: it may not be in our long-term interest.

An entirely different line of reasoning provides an additional argument for denying a sharp separation of human culture from nature. Almost all the landscapes that we see around us and call *natural* (and many of the seascapes) are products of human activity, often a result of intrusive management. Box 2.1 gives an example of a national park for birds that was "artificially" created by human cultural choices, and what happened to it when an attempt was made to let it revert to a more "natural" state. As we shall see later, the human-bereft so-called wildernesses of neo-Europe were typically created by the forcible expulsion of the First Nations.[12] Today, even

Box 2.1   Keoladeo Ghana National Park, India[11]

Keoladeo Ghana National Park is situated in Bharatpur, 50 km from the north Indian city of Agra (famous for the Taj Mahal). The main attraction of the park is a 450 *ha* human-made wetland with shallow bodies of water that was created by the local rulers (the maharajahs of Bharatpur) in the nineteenth century. The wetland was created as a reserve for hunting birds. More than 375 resident and migrant bird species have been recorded in this relatively tiny wetland. It both attracts thousands of wintering waterfowl and supports the large numbers of bird species that breed during the monsoon. It is the last place in south Asia where the presence of the migratory Siberian Crane (*Grus leucogeranus*) was recorded. Until Indian independence in 1947, the area continued to be a hunting reserve and was also used as a grazing ground for cattle (mainly buffaloes) from the surrounding villages and as a water source for irrigation during the dry post-monsoon period. After independence, it was set aside as a bird reserve and, after 1981, as a national park.

On the advice of Indian and US experts, who had not bothered to carry out systematic field studies, grazing was banned in the early 1980s in an effort to promote bird diversity. It was simply taken as obvious that the wetland would return to an even more species-rich natural state. When villagers protested the loss of fodder, the Indian state responded with violence and police killed nine protesters.

Despite its intent, the ban on grazing devastated Keoladeo as bird habitat. Paspalum grass and other opportunistic weeds, which had been kept in check by grazing, established a stranglehold on the wetland, choking the shallow bodies of water. Fish populations declined, leading to corresponding declines in bird nesting and sizes of bird populations. These results were presented in a 1987 report prepared by the Bombay Natural History Society, India's leading conservation NGO. The Society was one of the organizations that had originally promoted the ban and, to its credit, it changed its position in the face of recalcitrant data. Officially, the ban on grazing has never been reversed but it is no longer enforced. As a result some (technically illegal) grazing has resumed, and anecdotal reports suggested that in the late 1990s bird habitat was substantially improving. In the 2000s, however, the habitat came under sustained threat because of a decision to decrease the amount of water annually supplied to maintain the wetland, though recent reports (from 2008) are more promising.

the two Poles are in some danger of melting because of global climate change induced by human over-consumption. At best, the difference between the natural and the cultural is a matter of degree.

This does not imply that we may not consistently promote natural values distinct from those that produce urban sprawl, contaminated surroundings, or species-depauperate habitats. Even if humans are conceptualized as part of nature, we can coherently distinguish between humans and the rest of nature. There is at least an *operational* distinction; that is, one that we can straightforwardly make in practical contexts. We can distinguish between anthropogenic features (those largely brought about by human action) and non-anthropogenic ones. This is a critical distinction because we can straightforwardly be held ethically responsible for anthropogenic features; for instance, ongoing climate change. In contrast, we are not in the same way ethically culpable for the effects of a non-anthropogenic feature of the world, say, an earthquake or volcanic eruption, if we have done all we could to mitigate those of their impacts over which we have control. We do not have control over volcanic eruptions or asteroid impacts.

Moreover, a difference in degree, if large enough, may be of as much importance as a qualitative difference of type.[13] The human impact on nature may be so severe, because of its extent or because of its speed (or both), that it makes sense to make an operational distinction between humans and the environment, with *environment* being construed as the non-human part of nature. It is quite likely that species extinctions due to anthropogenic habitat transformation are having this type of severe impact. We know that anthropogenic climate change is almost certainly an impact of this severity.

The severity and speed of ongoing global warming has led the popular writer Bill McKibben to suggest that we are witnessing the end of nature.[14] *Nature,* in this construal, is used to connote what the environment (following the usage introduced in the last paragraph) was when humans were still largely at the mercy of external forces of nature—storms, volcanoes, famines, *etc.* Humans remain subject to such forces; however, nowadays, these forces increasingly become overwhelming only because of a result of human activity. They are "artificial": according to McKibben we are witnessing the end of the *natural.* Whether or not we accept McKibben's interesting analysis—which is independent of whether or not we accept the reality of anthropogenic climate change—it provides additional reason to make a distinction between humans and the rest of nature while acknowledging that humans are part of nature.

In the rest of this book, the term *environment* will be used to denote the non-human part of nature. This usage is in accord with how the term is used in the various environmental studies today and by movements that call themselves *environmental.* But it does not cohere well with the use of the term in many other contexts; for instance, in genetics or psychology.

Natural Values

In the same spirit, *natural values* will be defined as those that promote the persistence and increase of non-human biota or enhance non-anthropogenic aspects of the physical environment. While environmental ethicists have seemingly endlessly debated why natural values should be promoted (see Chapter 3), it is quite surprising how little philosophical attention has been paid to the enumeration of these values. We will attempt to produce a taxonomy here, emphasizing the problems that are encountered along the way. While doing so, we will in some cases (*e.g.*, biodiversity) gloss over the normative basis for promoting these values, leaving that discussion to Chapter 3. However, it is important to note that the list below is not supposed to be purely descriptive; that is, simply an enumeration of values that have been promoted in practice: the enumerated values are supposed to have normative justification. They are values that deserve to be promoted (because of the reasons discussed in detail in Chapter 3). Five categories of natural value are usefully distinguished: biodiversity, welfare, fidelity, service, and wild nature. This list is not exhaustive: the pursuit of beauty may sometimes lead to the enhancement of natural values. But these five categories are probably the most important.

Biodiversity

Chapter 5 will deal with problems with the concept of biodiversity. For the time being it will suffice to assume that: (1) biodiversity has two major components, taxa and ecological communities (groups of interacting taxa occupying the same geographical location) and (2) the number of taxa or communities (that is, the richness) provides an adequate measure of biodiversity for our purposes here. Biodiversity thus refers largely to non-human parts of nature; promoting it is trivially promoting a natural value. Chapter 3 will explore the normative basis for promoting biodiversity conservation; here, it will be assumed that there is such a justification. The important point is that not all components of biodiversity are of equal importance: we do not care about rock doves (our feral pigeons, *Columba livia*) as much as we care about the critically endangered Bengal tiger (*Panthera tigris tigris*). Rather, in practice, promoting biodiversity as a natural value requires its contextualization. Six criteria have commonly been used for this purpose:

- *Vulnerability*:[15] The argument for valuing vulnerable taxa or communities is straightforward. Promoting biodiversity means preventing extinction of species, communities, *etc*. If this is one of our goals, we have no option other than to focus on vulnerable biota because these are the ones most likely to become extinct without our attention. There is room for argument as to whether it is wise social policy to allocate resources on biota that may disappear in spite of our best efforts, as opposed to allocating them to biota with better prognoses. But that does not affect the appropriateness of using vulnerability as a criterion for contextualizing biodiversity.
- *Rarity*: In many situations the rarity of biota can be taken as an indicator of vulnerability. In such cases, this criterion is not independent of the last one and has the same normative justification. But rarity need not reflect vulnerability. We may choose to focus on rare biota just because (by definition) they are unusual, and promoting biodiversity in general requires the protection of the unusual.[16]
- *Richness*: Restricting attention to communities, those that have many species may deserve special attention partly because their persistence will ensure the persistence of a large number of species. (There are many problems regarding the role of richness in biodiversity conservation; we will return to this issue in Chapter 5.)
- *Suitability*: It makes sense to support biota at a locale if that locale, because of its biophysical features, is particularly suitable for those biota. It also seems at least inefficient to promote biota in an area in which they have little chance of persistence because of biophysical factors. Environmental suitability is thus an obvious criterion to use to contextualize biodiversity.

- *Proximity to native range*: This criterion is controversial. All other factors being equal, local species should be given preference over non-local ones in many contexts; for instance, if they are endemic to that region. Not doing so will make the species vulnerable to extinction. This criterion has generated controversy because on many occasions it may reflect socio-cultural prejudices such as nativism rather than genuinely natural value. At least arguably, "alien," "invasive," *etc.*, are human terms that become metaphorical when introduced in ecological contexts. After all, species' migrations and range shifts are routine ecological processes. There is much reason for considerable caution when we interpret nature in human terms; we should worry about whether we are reifying cultural choices into "natural" categories.
- *Cultural role*: [17] Biota continue to play significant cultural roles in a wide variety of cultures around the world even though, in the near future, most people may end up living in a rapidly expanding global culture in which differentiated natural values may be of little importance. However, today, species continue to have totemic value and have other forms of religious significance. They are used for hunting and other forms of recreation that may be a significant part of a culture's self-perception. Biodiversity can justifiably be contextualized using the cultural role of biota. In practice, in the North, this is already routinely done when charismatic species are used to formulate conservation policy; for instance the Bald Eagle and the Whooping Crane in the United States. To avoid misunderstanding, a somewhat subtle point needs to be reiterated here: cultural values are obviously human values. When they are promoted, what is ultimately being promoted is human well-being. How, then, can their promotion be used as a criterion to identify natural values? The point is that our definition of natural value only required that their promotion results in benefit for non-human biota (or enhancement of non-anthropogenic aspects of the physical environment). It does not matter whether it also enhances human welfare or whether its basis is ultimately anthropocentric; that is, based on human values and interests. (This point will be

23

important in the discussion of productivity in the service category below.) This is yet another advantage of eschewing a hard culture–nature distinction.

Welfare

Intuitively, it seems obvious that the welfare of environmental features is a natural value; that is, it is often stated that something is "good for" the environment. However, defining welfare precisely is not straightforward. For non-human living individuals of species, if we allow evolutionary theory to guide our reasoning, we can give at least an approximate definition of their welfare: it consists of their persistence and reproduction. There are problems with this definition: biological individuals are not quite as easily individuated as we may think.[18] All dandelions in a field are likely to have developed from the same cell and have identical genotypes, much like an animal body—in that sense they comprise a single individual. A typical human body contains more non-human cells (of microorganisms) embedded within it than human cells. Does the welfare of an individual human being include the welfare of all these non-human cells? Moreover, welfare, as we are viewing it here, is a normative concept: to take guidance from evolutionary theory we would be endorsing the normative claim that what is favored by evolution is desirable at least in this context, and this requires non-trivial argument. Any such normative claim cannot be "derived" from a descriptive claim (as all scientific claims are): any attempt to do so results in the *is-ought* fallacy—we will return to this issue in Chapter 3. There is ample room for caution in associating evolutionary success with normative desirability, as the history of Social Darwinism and eugenics reminds us. Nevertheless, in spite of these foundational worries, we should probably accept that we have a clear enough concept of individual welfare in most of the circumstances we are likely to encounter. Some may even choose to argue that we can identify individual welfare without recourse to evolutionary considerations. Drawing on a tradition loosely going back to Aristotle and exemplified by Albert Schweitzer (see Chapter 3), they may argue that we have a sufficiently precise intuitive idea of when individuals flourish without drawing on any specific scientific claim.

By the time we get to communities, the situation is much more difficult: reproduction is typically not relevant though communities are known to seed other ones. Moreover, when we use persistence to define the welfare of communities, it is also far from clear that "welfare" is being used in anything more than a metaphor, referring really to the individuals comprising the community. (The same point becomes relevant if we want to refer to the welfare of a species or other higher taxa.) For both the communities and individuals of sexually reproducing species, there is an additional complication because succession and aging are part of "normal" development.

Given these complexities, it should be clear that the only identifiable measure of welfare is that for individuals of species, and also, more importantly, that enhancing such welfare is a promotion of natural value. For sentient animals, we may want to add an additional criterion: the increase of pleasure and the decrease of pain, as advocated by the animal rights and welfare movements. The issues become much more confused once we turn to inanimate nature. When we say that we are harming a river by damming it, or a mountain by mining it, is "harm" anything more than a metaphor? We will avoid these problems by restricting this account of welfare to individuals of non-human species even while acknowledging the difficulties mentioned earlier.

Fidelity

We may want a habitat to become similar to some other "reference" habitat. It will be assumed that the reference habitat has a significant complement of non-human biota or salient non-anthropogenic physical features (as restoration ecologists typically demand). Promoting fidelity to such a reference habitat is then clearly a promotion of a natural value if it requires the enhancement of such features. However, beyond the very broad characterization just given, how the reference state should be chosen remains a matter of interesting controversy. Restoration ecology demands historical fidelity; the motivation for, as well as problems with, this choice will be discussed in Chapter 6. However, consider the English residents of the Himalayan town of Darjeeling in India during the colonial era. They routinely tried to recreate English gardens filled with non-native species, often importing seeds from the United Kingdom. According to the definition used here this would still constitute the promotion of a natural value. So would creating Japanese rock gardens in the United States, as would the creation of a community (of species) never achieved without human agency—most tradition-al gardens typically fall under this category (see Box 2.2). So would keeping aquaria as a hobby. Even a pesticide-filled manicured lawn is not excluded. Fidelity will often pull in directions antithetical to many other natural values, in particular biodiversity.

Box 2.2 Exotic Plants in Nineteenth-Century English Gardens[19]

Gardens have a long and continuous history in much of Europe, with the aesthetic principles of their design evolving over time. In England, by the early nineteenth century, they were sup-posed to embody qualities that were "calculated for displaying the art of the gardener" (in the words of an influential theorist, John Claudius Loudon). This art soon included nurturing exotic plants brought back by ships from colonial outposts all around the world. Many plants did not survive the long ocean voyages from China, India, the Americas, southern Africa, *etc.* This problem was alleviated by the invention in the 1830s of the "Wardian case," in which the plants could be transported. Named after Dr. Nathaniel Bagshaw Ward (its inventor), such a case consisted of a box with transparent glass sides and top that maintained a constant environment inside. These cases turned out to be remarkably efficient for the transport of live plants through inclement weather. Many plants also found the English climate inhospitable. This problem was solved by the construction of extensive greenhouses, starting with one famous example in Bicton in Devon, built around 1820 and still standing. The construction of giant greenhouses depended on the availability of cast iron and glass, the manufacture of which was immensely improved during the nineteenth century. Perhaps the most famous of these was the Palm House at the Royal Botanic Gardens, Kew, built between 1844 and 1848. Boilers in the basement ensured that even tropical palms from Africa, the Americas, and Asia could survive next to each other. Note that such gardens (including, of course, all the plants outside the greenhouses) typically have a role of promoting biodiversity as a natural value. However, whereas the contextual identification of relevant biodiversity components for promotion is usually now defended on grounds of rarity or vulnerability, in the early nineteenth century it was implicitly based on a cultural preoccupation with exotic plants.

Service

Non-human biota provide a variety of services that are critical for human well-being. So do non-anthropogenic parts of the physical environment, but that is relatively obvious: the pursuit of clean air or clean water is obviously a natural value.[20] This does not mean that these services can only be offered by non-human biota and non-anthropogenic environmental features. Mangroves provide environmental security (see below) but so do sea walls. The point is that we may pursue some services through the enhancement of natural values as defined above. There are a variety of service values that may be pursued. We focus here on the services provided by non-human biota that are achieved by ensuring the persistence of these biota (and, thus, ensure that the associated goal has a natural value):

- *Productivity*: We may choose to try to maximize the desirable biomass production of a habitat, with "desirable" being construed as the type of biomass that we need. Agriculture, aqua-culture, plantation forestry, *etc.*, are typical practices of this kind. Even though we pursue them for our own benefits, that pursuit requires attention to the welfare of non-human biota: productiv-ity is, therefore, a natural value in this context. But there are many problems. Imagine a plantation, a regimented landscape of rows of palm oil trees, for instance, along the Pacific coast of Costa Rica, where they have replaced biologically rich lowland rain forests. Should the welfare of these plantations be regarded as a natural value? By the definition being offered here, it would. This does not mean that these plantations are preferable to rain forests. Rain forests have higher biodiversity than plantations and this may trump the productivity value of palm oil plantations. What this example underscores is that natural values may be in conflict with each other. There is worse to come. Imagine that the plantations grow genetically modified (GM) crops. Is their welfare still a natural value? That will depend on what we mean by "non-human biota." If we dismiss GM organisms as human artefact, then the welfare of GM crops will not qualify as a natural value. If we admit GM organisms as non-human biota, the opposite is true. Nevertheless, we still may give this value little weight. A GM crop plantation may be preferable to a strip mall but less pref-erable than even a depauperate non-GM pasture.

- *Environmental security*: A particularly important type of service provided by (non-human) biotic systems is security against weather-related harm. Wetlands help flood reduction. Mangrove swamps along coasts mitigate the effects of storms. These goals require the pursuit of the welfare of non-human biota.
- *Ecosystem services*: Besides productivity and security there are a host of other services provided by non-human biota. Forests may serve as carbon sinks. Wetlands may remove pollutants from water. Water stored in intact ecosystems may serve to replenish aquifers. Soil production may depend on biota. We discuss the enumeration and calculation of ecosystem services in more detail in Chapter 3.

Wild nature

The value of wild nature has been both defended and criticized vehemently within environmental philosophy. It has been a constant preoccupation of many Northern environmentalists, and has perhaps equally often been treated with disdain by those from the South. Even in the North there are differences between those from neo-Europe (especially the United States and Australia) and those from Europe, with the latter less keen to deify the call of the wild. The explanation could be sociological: those from much of the South and from Europe live in historically cultural landscapes in which "nature" is usually tended. Meanwhile, wild nature has routinely been abundant in neo-Europe, often enough because it was created by forcible eviction of the original human inhabitants (see the next section). If wild nature should be promoted, the associated value is clearly a natural value. But is there a sound normative basis for wild nature to be embraced as a value to be promoted? Two positions should be distinguished: (1) the pursuit of wild nature as a goal among many other natural and cultural goals and (2) the situation in which the pursuit of wild nature trumps all other values. Even if Southern (and other) critics are correct in claiming that the second position is ethically bankrupt (again, see the next section), the first is hard to dismiss from consideration. It is sufficient to include wild nature as a natural value. Note, however, that the pursuit of wild nature has been interpreted in two strikingly different ways:

- *Wildness*: Wildness refers to unpredictability; in the context of nature it refers to the ability of non-human entities to generate surprises and, perhaps, to evade human control. These entities thus show autonomy independent of human interests and control. It is what Bill McKibben takes to be the hallmark of the "natural" when he bemoans the end of "nature." It may well have been what Thoreau had in mind when he claimed, "In wildness is the preservation of the world." We will return to the question of the normative basis for the justification of the pursuit of wildness in the next chapter.

29

• *Wilderness*: A strong definition of "wilderness" is a habitat bereft of any human presence or influence. A somewhat weaker version, requiring only no permanent human presence and minimal human influence, is enshrined in the US Wilderness Act (see Box 2.3). A wild habitat need not be a wilderness: think of humans eking out precarious livelihoods in the Ganga delta of Bangladesh, which is prone to floods and storms. A wilderness, according to the strong definition, is always wild: when there is no human encounter, *ipso*

Box 2.3   The United States' Legal Definition of Wilderness

"A wilderness, in contrast with those areas where man [*sic*] and his works dominate the landscape, is hereby recognized as an area where the earth and its community of life are untrammeled by man, where man himself is a visitor who does not remain. An area of wilderness is further defined to mean . . . an area of undeveloped . . . land retaining its primeval character and influence, without permanent improvements or human habitation, which is protected and managed so as to preserve its natural conditions and which (1) generally appears to have been affected primarily by the forces of nature, with the imprints of man's work substantially unnoticeable; (2) has outstanding opportunities for solitude or a primitive and unconfined type of recreation; (3) has at least five thousand acres of land or is of sufficient size as to make practicable its preservation and use in an unimpaired condition; and (4) may also contain ecological, geological, or other features of scientific, scenic, or historical value" (Wilderness Act of 1964, §1131(c)).

facto, nature in a wilderness enjoys autonomy. But wilderness, according to the weaker definition, is not necessarily wild: humans have transformed many temperate habitats without permanent presence and with very little effort. Does the pursuit of wildness, usually interpreted as the preservation of wilderness, have a sound ethical basis? The next section will explore this question (and other issues connected with wilderness) in some detail.

Even zoos promote natural values as construed here; this account clearly is open to the criticism that it may be too permissive. Meanwhile, the virtues of this account should also not go unnoticed. It embraces the plurality of ways in which people have attempted to promote what they take to be parts of the world distinct from human artefact. It explains how there may be conflicts between the ways in which the pursuit of natural values may be construed without having to dismiss all but one of the competing claims. It forces us to recognize that we must negotiate between different values. And finally, let us return to a problem raised in the last section: that many apparently natural habitats (landscapes or seascapes) were created by human agency (recall Box 2.1). We can now rationalize this usage: natural habitats are those that promote natural values, whether or not their origin is anthropogenic. Being a natural habitat is a matter of degree. Every garden is a natural habitat. But there is a difference between Tivoli Gardens and the Sakteng Wildlife Sanctuary in the remote Himalayas of Bhutan, home to 50 rare or endemic species of rhododendron and the mythical yeti. The question is, how salient is this difference?

The Trouble with Wilderness

Few topics in environmental philosophy have been as controversial as the preservation of wilderness. The first point to note is that wilderness, as an object of desire—as opposed to "waste" lands to be tamed—is highly localized and of very recent vintage. The historian Roderick Nash put it this way: "Friends of wilderness should remember that in terms of the entire history of man's [*sic*] relationships with nature, they are riding the crest of a very, very recent wave."[21] Historians often trace the contemporary positive conception of wilderness back to European Romanticism, to ideas of the sublime of which we are supposed to stand in awe. These dreams matured in those European colonies that were depopulated after colonization for one reason or another, mostly through introduced disease in the Americas and through conquest and forcible evictions in many regions.

But, is there a defensible normative basis for the creation or preservation of wildernesses? Critics have leveled three types of argument against it. Some have argued that wilderness preservation is conceptually incoherent, many that it is empirically impossible, and most that it is morally flawed.

The conceptual incoherence argument comes in two versions:

(1) Wilderness preservationism is supposed to presume a strict separation of humans from nature because human influence on a habitat is supposed to be strictly banned while non-human influence is left entirely alone. But a strict human–nature distinction is a pre-Darwinian view that can no longer be sustained: humans emerged from the evolutionary processes that spawned all biota. The concept of wilderness is thus identified with an incoherent conception of nature. It is supposed to follow that wilderness preservationism is also conceptually incoherent. Proponents of wilderness preservation have an easy—and compelling—response, though one that is rarely used: they can claim to be using no more than an operational distinction between humans and the rest of nature. The reason that this response is rarely used is because wilderness preservationism is typically accompanied by several other claims that do not cohere comfortably with such a "shallow" view of nature: we will return to this issue when we discuss the ideology of deep ecology in the next chapter.

(2) To assume that some state can be *preserved* assumes that it would not change of its own accord. To the extent that any wilderness preservationist wants to defend this claim, the task is hopeless. One of the most important developments in ecology in the late twentieth century was the recognition that natural communities are dynamic entities that are almost

never in a state close to a non-changing equilibrium. Wilderness preservationism in this version seems to assume that there is a state of a place that must be preserved and, by definition, this must be done without continued human intervention. This is impossible. This is a fairly compelling argument though there is an obvious response: recall that the critical clause of the definition of wilderness, in the weak version, is the absence of permanent human presence or significant influence. We could interpret the preservation of wilderness simply to mean absence of continuous human presence or influence and let "nature" take its course.

The argument from empirical impossibility is more compelling. Recall that the definition of wilderness (Box 2.3) requires that it be "untrammeled by man [*sic*]." We may quibble about what "untrammeled" requires, but it is probably uncontroversial to say that an area is not untrammeled if its ecological structure (what biotic communities inhabit it) depends on what humans have done. It becomes almost impossible to find wildernesses. The fabled wilderness areas of north America were extensively modulated by First Nation practices, especially through the use of fire.[22] The Australian Aboriginal nations had a similar predilection. Tropical rain forests have almost always been home to large numbers of people. We cannot preserve wildernesses because there are none. The only way out is to weaken the definition of wilderness, perhaps by removing any reference to human influences in the distant past and restricting the definition to what is now happening or has happened in the recent past and there, too, requiring no significant human influence. While many wilderness preservationists today would probably endorse such an option, the details of what counts as "significant" human influence must be spelled out explicitly.

The moral argument simply boils down to an incontrovertible— and uncontroversially unfortunate—fact. Many of the so-called wildernesses, especially those protected using the National Park model (originating in the United States in the nineteenth century), were created through the forcible expulsion of under-privileged people from their homes. It was a travesty of justice. It has long been recognized that, until quite recently, the creation of the famed US National Parks, from Yellowstone to Yosemite to Big Bend, required the forcible eviction of First Nations almost always without any, let alone adequate, compensation.[23] In a scathing indictment of wilderness preservation from the 1980s, Ramachandra Guha has pointed out similar events that occurred during the creation of tiger reserves in the 1970s and 1980s as part of India's Project Tiger—an ambitious attempt to prevent extinction of that species.[24] There are many other such examples but we must be careful as to what they really show. They do show that the practice of wilderness preservation has typically been deeply flawed in the past. They do not show that wilderness preservation as a goal does not have a sound normative basis (a question to which we will return in Chapter 3). They also do not show that this goal cannot be followed without compromising our deepest ethical principles: for instance, we may be able, through adequate compensation, to convince residents to vacate a habitat to create a wilderness. In retrospect, the moral argument against wilderness preservation does not appear to be as compelling as the empirical one, even though it is the former that continues to be much more hotly contested.

Perhaps the most crucial conceptual point to be made about wilderness preservation is that it is distinct from biodiversity conservation, even though the two programs have many commonalities (see Table 2.1). Whether or not some component of biodiversity can persist in the presence of human activity is an empirical question. Keoladeo Ghana National Park (Box 2.1) was a good example of diversity being maintained through intrusive human use of the habitat. In contrast, in central Texas, human presence has been inimical to the survival of two endangered bird species, the Golden-cheeked Warbler and the Black-capped Vireo.[26] The importance of not conflating biodiversity conservation with wilderness preservation is underscored by the fact that this conflation is common. It is even seen, for instance, in the Rio Convention on Biodiversity: in Annex I, wilderness, bizarrely, is treated as a type of ecosystem.

Table 2.1 Convergence and Conflict between Wilderness and Biodiversity

	Wilderness Preservation	*Biodiversity Conservation*
Objective	Habitats without humans	Biological diversity at all levels of structural, functional, and taxonomic organization
Justifications[25]	Aesthetic Ethical	Intellectual interest Ethical Prudential
Implementation	National parks Wilderness areas	High-biodiversity regions under any compatible management
Obstacles	Economic development and interests Over-consumption Human encroachment Invasive technologies Disease	Economic development and interests Over-consumption Human encroachment Invasive technologies Disease Habitat fragmentation Human neglect
Strategies	Legislation Habitat purchase	Legislation Habitat purchase Conservation easements Community or private stewardship and management of biota

Notes

1. See the essay "Ideas of Nature" in Williams (1980, pp. 67–85).
2. See Dasmann (1959).
3. Latour (2004, p. 251n) has even argued that the French do not have a concept of an "ahuman" nature (irrespective of the question of what merits protection). Anthropologists, in general, suggest that such a concept of nature is never found in non-Western cultures.

4. For this history, and also a detailed discussion of reductionism, see Sarkar (1998a).
5. See the discussion in Wynne (1994).
6. Besides Sarkar (1998a), see Rosenberg (2006) and Sachse (2007).
7. On Hobbes, however, see Martinich (2005): for Hobbes, human life in the state of nature, rather than nature itself, was "brutish."
8. White (1967) gives a similar account but dates the separation to around 1000 CE, citing industrialization in the sense of the use of water power for a variety of purposes.
9. See Darwin (1871).
10. In particular, August Weismann (1889), the most important evolutionary theorist in the generation after Darwin, rejected the idea—see Sarkar (2007a) for this history.
11. This discussion is based on Vijayan (1987) and Sarkar (2005) with more recent information from Bindra (2008).
12. See Cronon (1996) and Sarkar (1999).
13. As Engels once perceptively remarked, in the context of developing a "dialectics of nature" to underpin Marxism, quantity may be transformed into quality in such situations.
14. See McKibben (1989).
15. This is the criterion most often invoked by conservation agencies including the World Conservation Union (IUCN, formerly known as the International Union for the Conservation of Nature and Natural Resources)—see Margules and Sarkar (2007).
16. For instance, the international NGO Conservation International (CI) puts an emphasis on endemic species because they are rare. However, endemicity can also be an independent criterion, as discussed in Chapter 5.
17. Maffi (2001) provides an entry into the voluminous literature on this topic that has emerged in recent years.
18. Wilson (1999) provides a perceptive discussion of this issue.
19. See Thacker (1979) for more detail.
20. Thus, we talk about "natural capital" that is being lost as a result of environmental destruction.
21. See Nash (1973), p. xii; for more on the earlier debate over wilderness, see Guha (1989a), Cronon (1996), Sarkar (1999, 2005),Woods (2001). Many of the more influential works are reprinted in Callicott and Nelson (1998); the best of the recent work is collected in Callicott and Nelson (2008).

22. For this history, see Pyne (1982).
23. Spence (2000) details this history.
24. Guha (1989a); see also Agarwal (1992) for more on Project Tiger and Dowie (2009) for far-ranging documentation of these problems throughout the South.
25. The problem of justification is taken up in Chapter 3, which is about environmental ethics.
26. Mann and Plummer (1995) provide detail (and an unsympathetic history of conservation efforts for these species).

3

Ethics for the Environment

Why protect the environment? This question is the focus of environmental ethics. Philosophers (and other writers on the topic) have advocated two widely different approaches. One consists of emphasizing the importance of a well-functioning environment for human welfare. This approach falls within traditional (human) ethics, which has long been explored by philosophers. The other approach holds that environmental features—other species, individual organisms, perhaps even rocks, streams, mountains, *etc.*—are also ethically relevant. A strong version of this view, and one that was once endorsed by many environmental ethicists, is that these environmental features have moral standing; that is, we may have moral obligations to them. This approach to ethics is particularly philosophically interesting because it attempts to extend ethics beyond its traditional (human) domain. Both approaches merit attention in this chapter. However, normative claims from non-philosophical discourses—for instance, religious works—are beyond the scope of this book.

Philosophers often distinguish between metaethics and normative ethics, though the distinction is controversial. Metaethics is supposed to be concerned with the meaning and status of moral thought, language, and practice. Normative ethics is supposed to be concerned with which things are right, wrong, good, or bad. Normative ethics is further subdivided into theoretical ethics and practical ethics. The former asks question such as "which types of acts are

Environmental Philosophy: From Theory to Practice, First Edition. Sahotra Sarkar.
© 2012 John Wiley & Sons Inc. Published 2012 by John Wiley & Sons Inc.

right and why?" while practical ethics is concerned with the evaluation of such questions for individual acts. These distinctions are well illustrated by an example from Dale Jamieson.[1] Consider the following sentence:

(*) It is wrong to kill animals for food.

If we are concerned with whether (*) is an assertion of a claim or an expression of an attitude, we are dealing with metaethics. Someone taking the former position (that is, interpreting (*) as a claim) is called a cognitivist. Someone arguing that it is only expressing an attitude, perhaps to prompt you to behave in a certain way, but not wishing to say that a meaningful statement has been made, is called an emotivist. If we are concerned with why (that is, on what grounds) we should accept such a claim (after already interpreting (*) as a claim), we are concerned with theoretical ethics. If we are concerned with whether we should kill a particular animal for food, we are dealing with practical ethics.

In many situations the distinction between metaethical questions and (normative) ethical questions is not as clear as it was in this example. Moreover, much of the traditional philosophical writing about ethics includes both metaethical and ethical claims that are not explicitly distinguished. An additional potential source of trouble is that many philosophers believe that metaethical positions constrain ethical claims and *vice versa*. Nevertheless, we will ignore metaethics here: if environmental ethics really is going to expand the horizon of traditional ethics (as in the second approach to environmental ethics distinguished above), then it may well be wise to avoid the notoriously difficult controversies of metaethics until we are clearer about what we are willing to accept at the level of normative ethics.[2]

There is also some good reason to believe that metaethical questions are largely beside the point when we are worried about environmental issues. Consider, for instance, the disputed metaethical position of *moral realism*: that moral claims state facts about the world rather than, say, attitudes of the speaker. Let us assume that moral claims place responsibility on us to act appropriately. Now consider the following claim:

(†) Endangered tigers should be protected at the highest possible level.

Clearly, we may have an interesting debate about whether the claim embodied in (†) is correct. That will largely be a policy debate invoking practical ethics. We may even want to question why endangerment of a species is morally salient. That would be a question of theoretical ethics. But is it really relevant to debate whether (†) states a fact about the world or the attitude of a person? It hardly appears to be so. But perhaps we should not move so fast: an advocate of the importance of metaethics may argue that a fact about the world may require us to approach disputes about tiger conservation in a different way than a claim about an individual's attitude. If someone did not want tigers to be conserved, and (†) is a factual claim, we would have to find a way to check whether (†) is true or not in our world. If (†) is a claim about an individual's beliefs, we would have to examine those beliefs to determine its truth. If (†) only expresses an attitude we may just have to appeal to the individual's emotive responses. In the 1970s many environmental ethicists apparently believed that tying environmentally appropriate claims, such as (†), to facts about the world was the best way to achieve environmental goals. This may explain some of the popularity that moral realism enjoyed in those circles.

Yet, the position (basing environmental arguments on moral realism) has problems. It may be the case that no fact about the world can ever give us reasons that we find compelling in guiding our actions. In the 1700s David Hume pointed out that an *is* (a fact about the world) does not imply an *ought* (a moral obligation); claiming otherwise is supposed to be the *is-ought* fallacy.[3] In 1903 G. E. Moore castigated what he regarded as the *naturalistic fallacy*: assuming that ethical concepts could be defined using descriptive (non-normative) ones.[4] There are many responses to these arguments but their force is hard to deny. Perhaps more importantly, there is empirical evidence against the claim that recognition of facts psychologically induces any obligations in us to act "ethically." In what is perhaps an extreme case, the neurobiologist Antonio D'Amasio has described a neurological condition under which an individual makes what appear to be conventional moral judgments but feels no compulsion to act on them.[5]

We will have to broach metaethical issues if normative claims we analyze depend on them. Fortunately, we will encounter no such example in this book though that does not preclude them ever occurring while thinking about the environment. We will focus on theoretical ethics below but practical examples will be used to illustrate the theory. In particular, we will consider arguments about intrinsic value in some detail. There are interesting metaethical arguments about whether at least some entities must have such value;[6] these provide an example of issues that are beyond the scope of this book.

Demand Value

The simplest position seems to be that we should protect the environment because a well-functioning environment is not only good for the prosperity of individual human beings but for the survival of *Homo sapiens*. Under scrutiny this position does not turn out to be quite as simple as it initially seems. First, we must distinguish between human beings alive now and future generations. The former obviously have moral standing. For the latter, the situation is not quite so simple. Future (non-overlapping) generations consist of future persons who do not exist now.[7] Is there any sense in which we can have ethical obligations to non-existent things, especially if who those future persons will be (in terms of what they value, desire, *etc.*) may change on the basis of what we do? Second, if we are talking about the future of *Homo sapiens*, while it is easy to understand individual well-being and the ethical obligations it may bring, it is far less clear that we understand the prosperity of a species in anything but a metaphorical sense.

We will return to the question of the well-being of species in the next section. The discussion here will be restricted to human individuals. Let us assume that we can resolve the philosophical issues surrounding the concept of future generations and our obligations to them.[8] After all, since the 1970s it has been common to embrace responsibility towards future generations in public policy debates. This means that the goal of enhancing the welfare of future generations has become the goal of (some) people alive today and, in that sense, is a present goal that influences what we do. In this rather mitigated sense—but that is all that we need here—achieving the welfare of future generations reduces to concern for the well-being of persons alive today.

Now, by definition, an entity has *demand value* for someone if that person has a *felt preference* for it.[9] Next, assume that any individual has—or at least should have—a felt preference for those things that directly contribute to the individual's welfare. The qualification "at least should have" is necessary because it is far from obvious that individuals' felt preferences do track entities that enhance their welfare. For instance, a person may have a craving for unhealthy foods or excess alcohol, which are hardly conducive to enhanced welfare. Note that this is a descriptive claim subject to empirical testing—and the available evidence is far from clear. In what follows we will accept this claim while we examine how far demand values can take us towards formulating an adequate environmental ethic.

From this perspective, an environmental feature has demand value when it directly contributes to human welfare. Economists sometime advocate direct estimation of demand values through contingent valuation using "willingness-to-pay" (WTP) elicitations; that is, by asking individuals how much they would be willing to pay for various actions such as a decision to preserve or enhance some environmental feature. In principle this is possible even though, in practice, WTP estimates can be notoriously unreliable. For instance, an individual may be willing to pay x to preserve some feature, A, and y to preserve some feature, B, when questioned separately but may balk at having to pay $x + y$ to preserve A and B. This particular inconsistency can be avoided by eliciting WTP data only after all potential actions have been enumerated. But there are other problems including the fact that many potential actions only arise sequentially, and some disappear over time, so that all of them can never be listed at any given point.

Indirect estimation may be used to derive the cost of an action from other established costs. For instance, during the last few years many economists have tried to estimate the value of services provided by ecosystems using direct, contingent, as well as indirect valuation techniques. Box 3.1 discusses one very ambitious such effort, which

---

Box 3.1   The Value of the Earth's Ecosystem Services[10]

Robert Costanza and twelve colleagues attempted to calculate a global estimate of the value of ecosystem services provided by natural habitats in the mid-1990s. They defined ecosystem function as "the habitat, biological or system properties or processes of ecosystems. Ecosystem goods (such as food) and services (such as waste assimilation) represent the benefits that human populations derive, directly or indirectly, from ecosystem functions." For simplicity they combined goods and services together in the operational definition of ecosystem services. They considered 17 categories of such services: gas regulation (in the atmosphere), climate regulation, disturbance regulation (of ecosystems), water regulation, water supply, erosion control and sediment retention, soil formation, nutrient cycling, waste treatment, pollination, biological control (of populations), refugia (for species), food production, raw materials, genetic resources, recreation, and cultural services. For each of these they synthesized a large body of work to include both market and non-market values. (The latter consist of economic value that does not automatically show up in market prices; for instance, the recreational value of a coral reef.) Much of this work used "willingness-to-pay" (WTP) data, especially to

---

estimate the non-market value. The Earth was divided into terrestrial and marine regions; the former was divided into nine habitat types (with further sub-divisions) and the latter was divided into open ocean and coastal habitats (with further sub-divisions for the coasts). For each of these habitat parcels, the average value provided per unit area was estimated using the data that were available, generally for small regions. These numbers were then multiplied by the total area of that habitat type to obtain an estimate of the habitat type's global contribution. The final estimate was 16–54 trillion (10^{12}) US dollars per year (in 1994 US dollars). When this value is compared to the global gross national product of 18 trillion US dollars, it appears staggering. Yet, as Costanza and his collaborators point out, the figures are almost certainly an underestimate for many reasons, including the fact that many services may not have been recognized or fully incorporated.

attempts a global synthesis of the value of environmental services provided by natural habitats.

Appealing to demand values may well be very effective in the pursuit of some environmental goals. For instance, the demand value associated with an environmental feature (for instance, the persistence of a fish species) may be directly related to some entity's sustainability (in this case, a fishery). Similarly, if the restoration of an environmental feature is directed to a resource, the demand value is easy enough to assess. But restoration may be directed towards the recovery of natural values such as wildness, to which it is far more difficult to attribute demand value plausibly. By the time we get to conservation of biodiversity, the situation is even worse. Proponents may point to the unexpected value of some rare species such as the Madagascar periwinkle (*Catharanthus roseus*), found in a disappearing rain forest, which contained alkaloids that provided treatments for a wide range of diseases ranging from hypertension to Hodgkin's disease and leukemia.[11] But skeptics can equally point out that not only is there no reason to believe that every taxon will be of some such value but some biodiversity may even have negative value: for instance the rain forests of the Republic of Congo, which harbored Ebola. Had those forests been destroyed, the argument would go, Ebola may have disappeared with them.

This is not to suggest that economists have not tried WTP elicitations for biodiversity. The results have not been methodologically convincing because of the problems noted above. For instance, an analysis of WTP data for the United States for just 18 rare and endangered species showed that the average US household was willing to pay 840 US dollars per year for their conservation, which is highly implausible.[12] Some fish species merited only six US dollars per year, but even this is not plausible. If there were about 100 million households in the United States (a reasonable estimate for the mid-1990s, when these elicitations were carried out), it would mean that the smallest amount that the United States was willing to spend annually for any rare or endangered species was more than 600 million US dollars. If only conservation were that easy.

The important point is not that WTP elicitations are notoriously unreliable. As noted earlier there are many other, generally more indirect, estimation protocols for demand values. Rather, the Ebola problem must be faced: it is simply not obvious that environmental features necessarily directly contribute to human welfare. Moreover, the question whether the felt preferences on which demand values are based truly track welfare will not go away. For many of our environmental goals we must look beyond demand values.

Intrinsic Value

One such strategy has been to attribute intrinsic value to environmental features. Before we begin systematic discussion, two points are worth noting:

(1) What bears value are entities—individual beings, states of affairs, *etc.*—with what these entities are depending on the normative theory being used. However, they bear value because of some property they possess. For instance, human individuals may bear value because of the capacity of reason or the ability to feel pleasure or pain; states of affairs may also bear value because of their ability to generate pleasure or pain.

(2) "Intrinsic" can be used in at least two distinct ways.[13] (a) Philosophers sometimes regard a property of an entity (such as an environmental feature) to be *intrinsic* for a variety of reasons. In our context, the most important is that it may be intrinsic because it is defined non-relationally, in the sense that no reference to an external entity is necessary for its definition. (b) An entity may bear *intrinsic* value because it does not get that value from its relation to some other value-bearing entity. It gets its intrinsic value from some other property (perhaps, but not necessarily, a property that is intrinsic in the construal (a)).

Obviously, an entity can have an intrinsic property (*pace* (a)), without bearing intrinsic value (*pace* (b)). Consider *Symbion pandora*, a species that was first discovered in 1995 in the bristles of the Norway lobster (*Nephrops norvegicus*). *S. pandora* is tiny (about 350 microns in length) and structurally complex enough that it had to be assigned to an entirely new phylum, Cycliophora. Thus, *S. pandora* has several properties—tiny size, structural complexity, *etc.*—that are intrinsic under construal (a). Now, biologists find the species quite interesting because of some of these properties—notably, the structural complexity. Thus, in this case, if this assessment by biologists is used to attribute value to *S. pandora* it is not yet shown that the species has intrinsic value (under (b)). Its value depends on the biologists.

It is probably entirely uncontroversial that environmental features have a multitude of properties that are intrinsic in the sense of (a). However, in environmental ethics what has been at stake is whether environmental features bear intrinsic value, as defined by (b), and why. In this debate, the contrast has usually been with an entity having *instrumental* value, when it derives such value because of what it contributes to some other entity. We will focus on this contrast because this debate has traditionally been central to environmental ethics even though there are other ways in which entities may bear non-intrinsic value.

Much of the following discussion will be directed at the intrinsic value of (non-human) species and higher taxa because they are central to biodiversity conservation; less attention will be given to individual organisms, and non-biotic entities will be ignored until the end of the next section. Most of the interesting philosophical problems with intrinsic value attributions have already arisen in this context. Environmental ethicists have been trying to produce credible arguments in favor of attributing intrinsic value to species since the 1970s. (These arguments are equally applicable to higher taxa.) Table 3.1 details seven of the best-known of these arguments. (The

Table 3.1 Intrinsic Value Arguments

Religious authority	Some authors such as the ecologist David Ehrenfeld cite religious authority in the form of textual claims to attribute intrinsic value to biodiversity constituents such as other species.[14]
Holistic rationalism	Many environmentalists, particularly in the United States, have been strongly influenced by Aldo Leopold's land ethic: "A thing is right when it tends to preserve the integrity, stability, and beauty of the biotic community. It is wrong when it tends otherwise."[15] Thus it is no longer ethically acceptable merely to consider individual organisms; rather, in a more holistic vein, it is ethically required that we consider the entire biotic community.
Identification	The well-known philosopher Arne Næss has argued that we should recognize the intrinsic value of other living beings because we are able to identify with them: "We tend to see ourselves in everything alive. As scientists we observe the death struggle of an insect, but as mature human beings we also experience our own death in a way, and feel

Table 3.1 (*Continued*)

	sentiments that relate to struggle, pain, and death."[16] This spontaneous identification is supposed to the source of intrinsic value. Apparently, the property that is the basis for the attribution is that of being able to induce identification in us.
Bioempathy	Baird Callicott, also a philosopher (and perhaps the best-known philosophical exponent of Leopold's work), attempted to provide a naturalistic foundation for spontaneous identification by noting that we are related to all other living organisms through our evolutionary history.[17] Consequently, we feel empathy with them. Because we attribute intrinsic value to ourselves, it is supposed to follow that we should also attribute intrinsic value to these other organisms, which are related to us.
Expansion of the moral circle	Not very long ago, in most Northern societies legal rights such as voting were restricted to white males with property. Over the years they have been extended to those without property, females, and people of color (the sequence varied in different places). According to proponents of animal welfare, this process should now continue, to extend rights to all sentient beings—those that can feel pleasure or pain. Continue the process further and we end up with the expansion of the moral circle to include other living entities and, eventually, non-living parts of the environment. Presumably, the expansion of the moral circle that we have already seen resulted from the recognition that the entities from the expanded realm share some property that is a basis for the attribution of intrinsic value to the entities that were already included. Consequently, we have no basis for not attributing intrinsic value to these other entities. For instance, at least "higher" animals (including all vertebrate species except, perhaps, fish) seem capable of feeling pain. If the ability to feel

Table 3.1 (*Continued*)

	pleasure and pain is what was used to attribute intrinsic value to human individuals, and inflicting human pain should be avoided as a moral choice, then animal pain should also be avoided. This is sufficient to underwrite the concerns of most animal welfare activists. However, relying on pleasure and pain will only take us so far; it will not take us to "lower" animals—that is, those with very rudimentary sensory organs—and it will not take us to plants. But the properties posited by the next two arguments may take us to all living organisms.
Conativism	In general, "conation" refers to willing or, more accurately, striving towards some goal. In our context it is generally interpreted more narrowly as referring to the "will to live." It may be plausible to attribute such a will to all living beings, with "will" interpreted biologically (recall the discussion of individual welfare in Chapter 2). It is easy enough to assume that death-avoidance is a trait generally favored during evolution. Recognition of such a will led some figures, most notably Albert Schweitzer, to develop a "reverence for life" ethic.[18] In any case, it should be clear that, if a will to live is taken to be sufficient to attribute intrinsic value, it can be used to embrace all individual living organisms.
Interests	Living organisms have interests (in the sense of Chapter 2). Conation, in its biological interpretation of will to live, gives rise to some such interests. However, so do some other features that are universal to living organisms, especially what we could call a will to reproduce (in analogy to the will to live). Since the time of Aristotle, philosophers have found it easy to talk plausibly about what it is for an organism to flourish or be harmed without reference to human interests or values. Darwinian

49

Table 3.1 (*Continued*)

---

reproductive fitness is one obvious measure of such an interest. The legal scholar Christopher D. Stone once used the plausibility of such interests to urge legal standing for trees and, less convincingly, other natural entities such as mountains, rivers, and lakes.[19] If intrinsic value attributions are based on the property of having an identifiable interest, it is clear that these attributions can be made for non-human entities.

---

last three arguments are not independent of each other.) The "argument" from religious authority need not detain us here. It is not a philosophical argument; besides, it will have no force for those who do not recognize that particular religious authority.

The holistic rationalism argument is so called[20] because it relies on the fact that humans are involved in myriad relations with other entities, such as other species, with which they form a larger whole; if it is rational to attribute intrinsic value to human beings, it is supposed to be irrational to not also attribute intrinsic value to these other entities. The argument is question-begging, raising more problems than it resolves. It does not logically follow (or even follow as a canon of rationality) that attributing intrinsic value to an entity, *A*, requires the attribution of intrinsic value to any entity, *B*, that satisfies some relation to *A*, even if that relation is something as biologically fundamental as common descent. The point just made applies equally to the bioempathy argument discussed below.

The holistic rationalism argument goes back to the ecologist, Aldo Leopold, who announced *ex cathedra* that the unit that is morally salient is the biotic community, not the individual.[21] As such, it is not even an argument. But we can ask why, thereby generating some semblance of an argument. We can ask why—even in the case of the individual—integrity, stability, beauty, *etc.*, are morally desirable. In fact, traditional (human-centered) ethics attempts to answer this question, not by using these properties but by using properties such as the ability of (human) individuals to feel pleasure or pain or to be rational, which are supposed to be morally relevant. The history of ethics abounds in arguments as to why these properties are more credibly used to generate moral claims. For instance, we may take sentience (here used as the ability to feel pleasure or pain) or rationality to be constitutive of what it is to be a moral being. Similar arguments are necessary for integrity, stability, and beauty, especially when we turn to biotic communities. Leopold and his followers are presumably convinced that these three properties are sufficient. Leave aside the question of whether they are even morally relevant properties at the level of the individual. At the level of communities these properties are not even easy to define. Is every community beautiful and, if not, are there some communities that we should not conserve for this reason? This seems implausible. We will return to problems of defining stability and integrity in later chapters. Suffice it here to note that most natural communities are not stable by any definition and the question of their integrity remains unresolved partly because of the vagueness of the concept.

Both the identification and bioempathy arguments rely on some presumed facts about human psychology and seem to fall afoul of the is-ought fallacy. Suppose, for the sake of argument, that Arne Næss is correct about our spontaneous identification with all other organisms and also suppose that Baird Callicott correctly explains this aspect of our emotional constitution by invoking evolutionary history. Nothing normative follows from these purely descriptive claims. Attributions of intrinsic value are interesting only insofar as they come accompanied by responsibilities we incur from such attributions. Even if we (or most of us) empathize with other living entities, all that it means is that many of us may be motivated to preserve some of them. But it puts no moral obligation on those of us who are not so motivated. Just because we share a common ancestry with a bacterium or a moth or a venomous snake does not impose any moral obligation on us to protect or destroy them. To get to these obligations, some additional normative considerations beyond descriptive facts about our emotional responses are necessary. Again, these have not been forthcoming.

The final three arguments are much more compelling and will be treated together. They are also related to each other. The first asks for an expansion of the moral circle, and relies on sentience. The last two also ask for such an expansion but rely on other criteria. Recalling the discussion of welfare as a natural value in Chapter 2, let us assume that we can approximately establish what constitutes individual welfare for organisms. Moreover, assume that an organism's interests are those that promote its welfare. If the property of having interests is used to attribute intrinsic value to some limited set of organisms (notably, human individuals), it can obviously be used to argue for the expansion of the moral circle to include a wider set. With respect to conation (that is, striving towards a goal), given the discussion of Chapter 2, being alive contributes to the welfare, and is thus an interest, of an organism. Conation can thus also be used to expand the moral circle. As has already been noted, this chain of reasoning easily leads to the concerns of animal welfare movements. If animals have interests that deserve moral respect, these must surely include letting them live. Growing and killing them for food, clothing, *etc.*, clearly constitutes a violation of their interests and, hence, is morally unacceptable. Of course, the chain of reasoning leads to all other organisms, not merely animals, and we are left with the problem of having to justify even growing and killing plants for food. Many conflicts will have to be negotiated and we will have to develop guidelines for this purpose. If we cannot, we may have to settle for eating only those fruits that may be consumed without harming their future reproductive capacities. It will not be an easy life (if at all possible) but, perhaps, the whole point of environmental ethics is to propose for us a radically different way of living. However, there is no reason to believe that adequate guidelines cannot be developed.

From the perspective of biodiversity conservation, however, these last three arguments spell serious trouble. There are two (related) problems:

(1) Conservation is concerned with species, higher taxa, communities—in fact, the entire biotic realm (see Chapter 5). Let us restrict our attention to species. (These arguments trivially carry over to other taxa, communities, and so on.) Individual organisms may have fairly well-characterized interests but it is hard to see what we could mean by referring to a species' interest independent of the interests of its individual members. As a population evolves, according to the interests of its individuals, a species may disappear in the sense that it may be transformed into a new species.[22] (This type of speciation is known as *anagenesis*.) Communities change over time from one type to another. Does this harm the interests of the initial community type? We may have been given an argument for attributing intrinsic value to individual organisms. But we have been given no basis for doing so to species, higher taxa, communities, *etc.*, which are the focus of our attention when we try to forge an ethic in defense of biodiversity conservation. There is worse to come.

(2) Protecting one species may require deliberate harm to the interests of another. Protecting endangered sea turtle (Chelonia spp.) nesting sites along the Caribbean coast of Costa Rica requires trapping, and sometimes killing, dogs, which dig up and eat the turtles' eggs.[23] In South African national parks, protecting the habitat requires removal of elephants (*Loxodonta africana*), which used to be achieved efficiently by selective culling. Northern funders have banned such culling in recent years with devastating consequences to the habitat. Pursuing conservation forces uncomfortable choices. Once again, guidelines will have to be developed to negotiate conflicts but, this time, we cannot fall back on individual interests—the difficulties noted in (1) return with a vengeance.

Where does this leave us? We may have good arguments for attributing intrinsic value to individuals of non-human species. (None of the arguments we have encountered take us to non-living entities.) If we endorse attributions of intrinsic value on the basis of the ability to feel pain and pleasure, we can attribute intrinsic value to many animals but not other organisms. If we base it on the ability to have identifiable interests, we may attribute intrinsic value to all living individual organisms but this gives us a difficult program of figuring out how to live ourselves without wanton harm to many such interests. In any case, we do not have an ethic that justifies either a focus on species, higher taxa, communities, *etc.*, or many measures that are necessary for conservation.[24]

The last point also underscores an occasionally unavoidable conflict between animal welfare and biodiversity conservation.[25] As we saw earlier, concern for animal welfare would discourage the culling of dogs in Costa Rica or elephants in South Africa, whereas biodiversity conservation encourages such measures. Depending on the sense in which we view conservation biology as a science, and we will return to this question in detail in Chapter 5, there is a sense in which it may *require* such measures. The point is a little subtle. If we view conservation biology as a science like ecology, unconstrained by cost considerations, there are many ways to remove the dogs and elephants without culling; for instance, by relocating them somewhere else. (For the sake of argument, we will assume that this will not harm, or at least significantly harm, their interests.) However, if we assume that conservation biology operates under resource constraints, given that societal resources for conservation are finite (and often relatively small), then the problem to be solved becomes one of constrained optimization: what is the optimal way to expend resources to achieve the desired goal—in this case, the reduction of the dog or elephant population? The answer may well be culling. We may, of course, move beyond biodiversity conservation and embrace the goal of animal welfare. Then we may add a new constraint to the optimization problem: culling is not a policy option. However, such a move would only underscore the potential for conflict between animal welfare and biodiversity conservation.

We will now turn to yet another strategy for justifying ethical concern for the environment. We will return again to the question of intrinsic values in Chapter 9.

Transformative Power[26]

Intrinsic value arguments did not get us as far as we may have hoped toward a satisfactory environmental ethic, at least if the latter is to include an ethic for biodiversity conservation. Can instrumental value do any better, with the instruments wielded for human interests? Luckily, most of us believe that there is more to human welfare than what can be captured by demand values traded in the marketplace. Except, perhaps, in some areas of north Africa, it is taken for granted today that human liberty must not be traded in the marketplace and, even where slavery exists, it is almost always officially illegal. While some cultures endorse trading sex for money, even in those cultures most individuals would probably prefer less of such a trade. Most religious individuals would probably not want religious experience and entities of religious significance to be traded in the marketplace. There is more to us than felt preferences that we are willing to trade. In particular, we will rely in these arguments on those experiences that can transform how we view life, including changing our felt preferences.

Bryan Norton introduced the (presumably hypothetical) case of a young girl who is presented with a ticket to a classical concert.[27] She has no previous exposure to classical music and, as a result, has no interest in it. She would not be willing to pay anything at all for such a ticket. For her, the ticket has no demand value. On a whim, she goes to the concert. She enjoys it so much that her world is transformed. In the future she will be willing to pay a considerable amount of money to hear classical music. Her demand values, depending on her felt preferences, have been transformed.

What this example is supposed to show is that entities that have no demand value may yet have transformative power. Such cases are not hard to find. Think, for example, of any old cylindrical piece of rock that may end up being worshipped by Hindus as a phallic manifestation of their god, Siva. Environmental goods that may acquire their status as meriting normative concern include biodiversity and wilderness, both of which will be discussed in some detail below. In the literature of environmental ethics, such entities were said to have transformative *value*. However, the pursuit of these entities cannot be calibrated using a valuational framework such as the WTP procedures discussed earlier or other parts of the framework of decision theory discussed in Chapter 4. In fact, it is not obvious that entities that can transform our world views in this way can even be ordinally ranked (that is, qualitatively arranged in a linear order), let alone be measured in a quantitative scale (which would assign numerical values to each entity). Though doing ethics does not require that all values must be capable of being ordered, let alone quantified, it nevertheless seems less confusing to attribute transformative *power* rather than *value* to entities of this sort.[28] (It will also ensure that the terminology used here will remain consistent with that of the rest of this book.)

There can be a plurality of ways in which entities can have transformative power. For instance, biodiversity may have transformative power because of an individual's experience of new and interesting habitats. Purveyors of ecotourism rely on this appeal. Sometimes, as in the case of television shows such as the Nature Channel or National Geographic (in the United States), even vicarious experiences may suffice. But biodiversity also has a more powerful transformative effect because of what it has meant and continues to mean for science. Close observation of the diversity of life led Darwin and Wallace to formulate the theory of evolution by natural selection—one of the most significant human intellectual achievements ever, and one that transformed even how we view what it is to be human. Biodiversity continues to contribute to evolutionary biology and ecology today.

Similarly the appeal of wild nature—both wilderness and wildness (recall Chapter 2)—may also largely result from its transformative power. The sublime in nature, of which we are in awe, even more than the beautiful, transforms how we think, perhaps by reminding us of our relative insignificance in the order of nature. The religious may well be reminded by wild nature of the presumed power of their gods. Thus, once again, the transformative power of wild nature can arise in a plurality of ways. Many wilderness enthusiasts seek spiritual solace in the solitude of wilderness, though, in this respect, Thoreau seems to have been satisfied merely with nature's wildness available around him, even close to human settlements.[29]

What holds for sublime nature also holds for historical and religious monuments and other works of cultural significance. For advocates of an ethic based on the transformative power of entities, we should protect such artefacts because of their transformative power, just as we should protect relevant aspects of nature. There may be some irony here: the justification for protecting biodiversity and wild nature may end up being the same as that for protecting the most profound products of culture. But there is no inconsistency. The discussion here should not be taken to suggest that arguments based on attributions of transformative power are entirely without problems. Table 3.2 discusses two of the most obvious objections: the boundary problem and the directionality problem.

Table 3.2 Objections to Transformative Power Arguments

Boundary problem	A self-styled mystic may claim to have had a transformative experience from a blade of grass. Indeed, the individual in question may genuinely have had such an experience, like Antoine Roquentin in Sartre's novel, *Nausea*. The blade of grass then has transformative power. Should we, then, protect it? In principle, yes. But we have the problem that we do not know how to draw a boundary that only includes those entities that have transformative power and excludes all others. For instance, it is no secret that psychedelic drugs have transformative power. We may be called upon to protect all and anything that anyone feels may have transformative power for someone. How should we draw the line? The only answer—and it is not a very convincing one— seems to be that it would be wise to focus on the sorts of entities that have routinely been known to have transformative power. We may miss the

Table 3.2 (*Continued*)

---

	mystic's blade of grass but, in practice, such cases are probably rare.
Directionality problem	Not all drug experiences are pleasant and lead to desirable transformations in an individual. It is obvious that not all entities with transformative power should be tolerated, let alone actively encouraged to persist or even flourish. Exposure to wild nature is not always positive: a near escape from a predator or from a dangerous fall may result in an individual becoming imbued with fear of all non-artificial surroundings. Biodiversity may present itself in the form of recalcitrant parasites. But even drug experiences can have powerful positive effects; for instance, in societies accustomed to the ritual use of drugs. Three separate but related problems should be distinguished. (1) Nothing in the account of transformative power ensures that the experienced transformations are positive or negative. In other words, we need an independent set of criteria that specify which experiences result in positive transformations. The only obvious option seems to be that of relying on past experiences to decide which type led to positive transformations. (2) If we take this option, we need a method to determine which experiences are desirable. This method must itself be justifiable and, moreover, cannot simply fall back on felt preferences. Otherwise we have not gone beyond demand values. (3) As in the examples given above, the same experience may turn out to be positive or negative depending on a variety of contingent factors. There may well be no experience that always produces positive transformations. In other words, proponents of transformative power arguments have a lot of work left.

In this context, let us finally return to the question of whether non-biotic environmental features such as mountains and rivers can have intrinsic value. Consider a possibly analogous claim: Angkor Wat (or pick your favorite monument or piece of art) has intrinsic value. The analogy does not appear to be forced insofar as neither a mountain nor such a non-living human artefact have properties associated with living things. The real question to ponder is whether the claim of intrinsic value is meant to do any more than to suggest that the value of such an entity is beyond the demand value that can be established in the marketplace. Suppose that Ted Turner managed to buy Angkor Wat from some impoverished Cambodian regime in the future. Does this give him moral authority to dismantle it, or paint it with lurid colors in the way he colorized the film classics he bought several decades ago? Presumably not, but this conclusion can also be reached by attributing transformative power to Angkor Wat. In other words, if intrinsic values are only supposed to move us beyond the domain of the market, then there is no need here to endorse attributions of intrinsic value. Recalling the transformative power of wild nature, and noting the similarities with non-biotic environmental features (even when these are not associated with wild nature), we leave this section by noting that attempts to attribute intrinsic value to rocks, mountains, rivers, *etc.*, *may* be no more than attempts to recognize their transformative power beyond demand values, whether or not they are established through market mechanisms.

Anthropocentrism, Biocentrism, and Ecocentrism

These three terms all refer to "ideologies" that lie behind some theoretical normative claims that are popular with certain brands of environmentalists. ("Ideology" is used here to refer to wide-ranging general sets of beliefs that include a normative component; nothing pejorative is intended by the use of the term.) All three terms are routinely encountered in environmental philosophy, though "bio-centrism" and "ecocentrism" are not always distinguished from each other or in the same way. For future reference it is worth at least informally defining these terms and connecting them to the other issues discussed in this chapter. We will not attempt any evaluation of them because each is too diffuse for succinct treatment.

Anthropocentrism presumes that all values are ultimately based on human values. Attributing intrinsic value to non-human entities is anathema to this position. Any position that presumes that all values must be reducible to demand values obviously falls within the rubric of anthropocentrism. Embracing entities with transformative power goes beyond such reducibility to demand values; this position is sometimes called weak or tempered anthropocentrism.[30]

Biocentrism presumes that we should include all individual living entities in our moral considerations.[31] Thus, it is permissible to attribute intrinsic value to all of them. Conversely, if we attribute intrinsic value to all such entities, we are committed to biocentrism. Biocentrists sometimes criticize anthropocentrists as "speciesists," with that term intending to inherit the type of moral opprobrium associated with racism or sexism. They are also often uncomfortable with views—associated, for instance, with Peter Singer and many other proponents of animal welfare[32]—that would restrict moral consideration only to sentient beings, leaving out other living beings.

Ecocentrism goes further than biocentrism and brings (1) collectives such as species and sometimes also (2) non-biological natural features of the world such as rocks, mountains, and rivers into the moral sphere.[33] We are supposed to owe them moral consideration because they are related to us. Whether this is true in any interesting sense of "related," especially in case (2), remains questionable. But, even if it is, this argument suffers from the same problem as the argument from bioempathy discussed above: it does not have any automatic normative implications. It does not logically follow from our being related to some entity that we owe it moral consideration.

The Long Shadow of Deep Ecology[34]

During the last quarter of the twentieth century, environmental philosophers hotly debated an ideology called "deep ecology," which was also often endorsed by many conservation biologists from the North and held in equal disdain by most environmental scientists (including social scientists), philosophers, and activists from the South. For the sake of completeness we note a few aspects of this ideology even though it is questionable whether it is of any philosophical interest (as opposed to political interest stemming from its role in the emergence of several Northern environmental movements).

The origins of deep ecology lie in the Norwegian environmentalism of the late 1960s and early 1970s. The ideology comes in two versions, both prominently associated with the philosopher Arne Næss.[35] The original Norwegian version distinguished itself from what it called "shallow ecology," which focused on immediate material goals such as resource depletion and pollution, which were held to be of primary relevance only to Northern societies. In contrast, deep ecology demanded a focus on the long-term future of the environment and emphasized issues of equity and justice, including the welfare of Southern societies.

All these social concerns disappeared from the second version of deep ecology, which replaced the first in the 1980s and was developed primarily in the United States.[36] This manifestation of deep ecology instead actively opposed anthropocentrism and embraced biocentrism/ecocentrism. Much of its critique was directed against "humanism," with its concern for human interests. The second version of deep ecology deified the intrinsic value of non-human environmental features (which the earlier version had also endorsed).[37] At the metaphysical level it emphasized holism or the alleged interconnectedness of everything with everything else. Thus, all entities emerged as potential objects of ethical concern. As matters of policy, many of deep ecology's adherents argued for strict wilderness preservation and human population reduction.

However, deep ecology's influence was mainly seen outside academia, where it often inspired radical activism in defense of the environment, whatever that was supposed to mean. More controversially, deep ecology inspired millenarian movements in the

North, such as Earth First! in its early days.[38] At its most extreme it opposed poverty alleviation and famine relief on the grounds that a decrease in human population would benefit the environment. In the 1980s, one of its proponents, Dave Foreman (a founder of Earth First!), welcomed the famine in Ethiopia because it would decrease the number of human beings. (He subsequently publicly retracted this position.[39]) On similar environmental grounds, deep ecologists often objected to immigration from the South to the North (recall the discussion in Chapter 1). Deep ecology's influence continues to be felt in such fringe movements as the Wildlands Project, which seeks to restore most of North America to its Pleistocene past. We will return to this example in Chapter 6.[40]

Notes

1. The discussion here follows Jamieson (2008).
2. For more development of this point, see Elliott (2001) and Sarkar (2005).
3. See Hume (1972 [1737]).
4. See Moore (1903); Frankena (1939) discusses the relation between the naturalistic and the is-ought fallacies.
5. D'Amasio (1994) describes this example in detail.
6. See Jamieson (2008) for a detailed discussion.
7. For an influential discussion of future persons, see Parfit (1984). Garvey (2008) has emphasized the importance of discussing this problem in the context of our moral obligation to future generations when we are responsible for climate change.
8. For more discussion of this issue, see Gosseries and Meyer (2009).
9. For a more detailed discussion of problems with demand values in the context of environmental ethics, see Norton (1987).
10. This is based on Costanza *et al.* (1997).
11. Caufield (1984), p. 220.
12. On contingent valuation of endangered species, see Loomis and White (1996).
13. The discussion here follows Sarkar (2005), Chapter 3.

14. See Ehrenfeld (1976), who found support for biodiversity conservation in Judaeo-Christian religious texts; White (1967) argued for the opposite position on his reading of the same texts.
15. See Leopold (1949), pp. 224–225; for an elaboration see Callicott (1989).
16. See Næss (1986), p. 506. The point is somewhat elaborated in Næss (1989).
17. See, especially, Callicott (1986).
18. See Schweitzer (1976).
19. See Stone (1974); Stone (1985) is a partial retraction.
20. This terminology originates from Callicott (1986).
21. See Leopold (1949), as discussed in Table 3.1.
22. Note that even a single (human) individual's interests may also change over the course of time.
23. These examples are discussed in more detail in Sarkar (2005) and are partly based on field work (Sarkar, unpublished data).
24. However, for a recent defense of intrinsic value arguments, see McShane (2007).
25. This point seems to have been first made explicitly by Callicott (1980).
26. The argument based on transformative value originated with Norton (1987). It was extended by Sarkar (2005). The term "transformative power" is introduced here instead of "transformative value" because it seems more appropriate—see the discussion later in the text.
27. See Norton (1987) for this example.
28. As noted earlier, this is a change from Norton (1987) and Sarkar (2005).
29. To quote Thoreau (from 1862), "in wildness is the preservation of the world."
30. See, for instance, Sarkar (2005).
31. Taylor (1986) is a classic statement.
32. See Singer (1975, 2001).
33. For example, see Wenz (1988).
34. The classic position is that of Næss (1989). There have been many debates over deep ecology, which are impossible to summarize easily. Drengson and Inoue (1995) is a useful anthology; Keller (2009) provides an update. Guha (1989a) is a particularly important critique. Ferry (1995) and Sarkar (2005) provide entries into the critical literature.
35. See Næss (1995 [1973]).
36. The contrast is seen in Næss and Sessions (1995 [1984]).

37. Indeed, for many adherents, especially those outside academia, an assertion of intrinsic value to non-human natural entities is the hallmark of deep ecology.
38. Lee (1995) provides an excellent history.
39. See Foreman (1991).
40. See Soulé and Terborgh (1999).

4

From Ethics to Policy

No matter what ethical norms we choose to embrace, if we want to be of practical help in solving or even ameliorating environmental problems, we must find a way to translate those norms into policy. This is typically not a trivial matter. Policy depends on both our values and facts about the environment that we can only glean from empirical work. The trick is to combine facts and values into appropriate decisions. We can do so intuitively, as we typically do in everyday life. Or we can employ the more systematic methods of decision theory, which result in the formulation of decision protocols: explicitly structured ways of developing and analyzing policy options.[1] In the public arena, the latter has the advantage of making it possible for our policy formulation process, especially our assumptions, to be critically analyzed by others, and gives us the opportunity to make corrections when appropriate. The process must be transparent. Decision theory is increasingly being used in environmental decision contexts because these decisions are typically made by governmental agencies, which are subject to external, especially public, scrutiny, which in turn often generates a legal requirement for transparency. In particular, decision theory is central to the project of systematic conservation planning for biodiversity, which will be discussed in detail in Chapter 5, and is one of the most extensively developed protocols used for environmental decisions. Decision theory is also philosophically rich, generating an unusually interesting class of apparently intractable philosophical

Environmental Philosophy: From Theory to Practice, First Edition. Sahotra Sarkar.
© 2012 John Wiley & Sons Inc. Published 2012 by John Wiley & Sons Inc.

problems.[2] It attempts to combine facts (along with the uncertainty about those facts) with values in a systematic way. This chapter will barely touch on the extensive problems of philosophical interest provided by decision theory; it will be restricted to those that are likely to be of practical relevance to environmental decisions.[3]

However, to combine facts and values in this way, decision-theoretic methods (and particularly formal methods) typically assume that values have been identified, individuated, and sorted properly; that alternative courses of action have been fully specified; and so on. When this is not true, more deliberation is necessary. One additional advantage of decision-theoretic methods is that they often make us recognize when we have not organized values and advantages properly by producing results that are clearly counter-intuitive given what we set out to do. Thus, formal methods may send us back to more deliberation and argument, which should lead to better decisions. This chapter will largely be about decision theory but, before we turn to that, we will take a cursory look at the source of the relevant facts—that is, the environmental sciences—and at the nature of uncertainty.

Environmental Sciences

There are many environmental sciences, both natural and social. Later chapters will address philosophical issues within conservation biology (Chapter 5) and restoration ecology (Chapter 6). There are many other environmental sciences, including ecological economics, environmental chemistry, environmental engineering, environmental microbiology, physical geography, toxicology—there is no point in trying to come up with a complete list given the range of viable interpretations of "environment" (Chapter 2). Rather, what is important here is an analysis of the contributions that the environmental sciences are supposed to provide for making policy decisions.

Table 4.1 summarizes what we may expect from the environmental sciences. An important point is to recognize that what will be taken to be *scientifically* relevant may depend on societal values. For

Table 4.1   Input from the Environmental Sciences

Assessment of the status of an environmental problem	The relevant science would provide a model that predicts what would happen if no action is taken. In principle this appears straightforward. However, prediction in the ecological and social sciences depends on so many variables that precise prediction of outcomes is often impossible. Hence the importance of quantitative uncertainty assessments, discussed below.
Design of policy options	The environmental sciences help in designing scientifically viable policy options, which are the alternatives available to decision makers. Once again, accurate prediction is an issue that must be explicitly treated.
Assessment of the consequences of each policy option	The environmental sciences should provide tools to predict the outcome of each policy option. Note that taking no action is also a policy option: in that sense the status assessment stage above can be subsumed under this stage. If all consequences of policy options are judged unsatisfactory (which is not a purely scientific issue), then we must return to the design stage and formulate more policy options.
Estimates of the uncertainties of each assessment	A highly desirable policy outcome may have a very low probability. A somewhat less desirable outcome may have a much higher probability. We may (but need not) choose the latter alternative. It is not the task of the environmental sciences to decide between such differences; it is ratherthe choice of social policy. However, what the environmental sciences should do is specify how probable each policy outcome is, preferably quantitatively.

instance, are we interested in how much of a natural habitat will be lost to urban sprawl? Or how much habitat will be left for a bird species of local interest? Or the amount of lead that will be released into the groundwater by a new industrial plant? Focusing on any of these parameters is a cultural (or societal) choice. That cultural choices are involved in limiting (or encouraging) urban sprawl is obvious. When it comes to the welfare of species (or other biota), as we shall see in detail in Chapter 5, cultural choices are involved in selecting which entities deserve our explicit attention. When it comes to deciding how much lead contamination we are willing to tolerate, let us suppose that the environmental sciences provide a robust estimate of the health risks associated with each lead level in the groundwater. It still remains a cultural choice to determine what level of risk is deemed socially acceptable. We have to establish norms defining acceptable risk—which goes beyond the descriptive estimates provided by risk analysis.

Predictions in science come from models that incorporate within them assumptions about what entities exist and how they interact with each other. We will take models to be "low-level" theories; that is, theories with a limited scope of applicability.[4] With this usage, a general theory of species' competition is simply a broader model (of wider scope) than individual models of species' interactions limited to a few species. Philosophers have often construed the model–theory relationship in other ways (and there is a vast literature on this topic) but this characterization will suffice for our purposes.

One important source of difficulty in this context is the complexity of most environmental interactions that are relevant to policy, particularly when human agency must also be incorporated into models. In practice, models cannot incorporate every entity and interaction; otherwise they would become intractable and practically irrelevant. Rather, modelers must choose those entities and interactions that they believe to be most salient. Different modelers may make distinctive but plausible choices, leading to different models. In principle, which choice is the most appropriate should depend on epistemological criteria, the most important of which is predictive success. The trouble is that, when complex systems are modeled, no model typically outperforms all others in all contexts. Nevertheless, as our computational capacities increase, model predictions typically improve even in the face of overwhelming complexity. Box 4.1 illustrates these issues in the context of models of climate change.

Box 4.1   Climate Change Scenarios and Models[5]

Global warming was identified in 1896 by the Swedish chemist Svante Arrhenius, who recognized that anthropogenic production of carbon dioxide can raise the temperature of the Earth by blocking the solar radiation reflected back into space by the Earth's surface. However, it was only in the 1950s that it was recognized that relatively small increases in the amount of carbon dioxide can lead to significant increases in temperature. Almost simultaneously it was also recognized that the oceans did not have the capacity to absorb as much anthropogenically produced carbon dioxide as was previously believed. From the late 1950s and 1960s scientists began to track carbon dioxide concentrations in remote areas (far from sources of pollution) in Hawaii (on the top of a mountain, Mauna Loa) and in Antarctica. They found a steady increase. Meanwhile, scientists also began to reconstruct past atmospheric compositions, especially from air bubbles trapped in the Greenland and Antarctic ice sheets.

Atmospheric carbon dioxide was about 200 ppmv (parts per million by volume) during the last Ice Age (20 000 years ago), had risen to about 280 ppmv by the beginning of the Industrial Revolution (around the year 1750), and had risen again to about 370 ppmv by the end of the twentieth century. Meanwhile, the global mean temperature increased by about 6°C between the last Ice Age and the beginning of the Industrial Revolution. Much of this increase is due to the change in the Earth's orbit around the Sun, which took us out of the Ice Age. The well-established historical correlation between carbon dioxide levels and rise in temperature—and the existence of a "greenhouse" mechanism, which shows how carbon dioxide achieves this effect by blocking radiation from leaving the Earth—implicates carbon dioxide as being responsible for part of the historical increase and almost all of the recent increase in temperature: about $0.65 \pm 0.05\,°C$ since around 1850 and $0.2–0.3\,°C$ since around 1950. Now, carbon dioxide is not the only or the most efficient greenhouse gas. Water is also effective, and methane much more so than carbon dioxide. But water levels in the atmosphere have not varied systematically and greenhouse gases such as methane are far lower fractions of the atmosphere. Consequently, carbon dioxide is the most important of the anthropogenically produced emissions implicated in creating global warming and, through it, climate change.

What are worrying are the implications of global warming and climate change for the future. If levels of greenhouse gases rise, so will the temperature on the surface of the Earth. Even a rapid increase of a few degrees will have devastating effects on human well-being, especially in the most disadvantaged communities of the South; for instance, by raising sea levels, making precipitation patterns more uncertain, and possibly also by encouraging more extreme climate events. The negative effects on some forms of biodiversity—for instance, coral reefs—may be equally severe. Skeptics used to argue either that global warming was not happening, or that it was not anthropogenic, or that the effects will somehow be balanced by the Earth's response. Such skepticism was almost always politically motivated, serving the interests of the fossil fuel industry and, by now, has no scientific credibility.

The work of the Intergovernmental Panel on Climate Change (IPCC) was crucial in establishing the scientific claims about climate change that are now considered definitive. This body was created in 1988 jointly by the United Nations Environmental Programme and the World Meteorological Organization to investigate the status of global warming. It involves a collaboration between hundreds of scientists and has produced detailed periodic assessments that represent the scientific consensus at the time. The most recent assessment is from 2007 and the discussion here will be based on it. We will not focus on the IPCC's acceptance of ongoing anthropogenic climate change, which is obvious. Rather, we will look at how the IPCC tries to predict the future using sophisticated model-based analyses. These analyses must cope with the overwhelming complexity of the climate system, which is affected by interactions between many factors, including the Sun and physical changes in it, the land and water on Earth's surface, cloud formation and behavior, vegetation and other land cover change, and various human actions including fossil fuel consumption.

In 2000 the IPCC produced a "Special Report on Emissions Scenarios," which analyzed four important possible "storylines" or families of scenarios of what humans will do in the near future. The emphasis was on how energy needs would be met. These were:

- *A1*: There is supposed to be very rapid economic growth. The global population is supposed to peak in the middle of the twenty-first century and decline thereafter. The emphasis is on rapid technological change. Increasing globalization is supposed to take place, with progressive equalization of regional *per capita* incomes.
- *A2*: This family describes a very heterogeneous *non-global* world, with preservation of local identities and an emphasis on local self-reliance. Regional fertility patterns converge only slowly, resulting in the continued expansion of the global human population. Economic development is also locally oriented and *per capita* economic growth continues to have significant disparities between regions and is generally lower than in other storylines.

71

- *B1*: This family includes a convergent world with the same population assumptions as *A1*. However, it is supposed that there are rapid changes in economic structures leading to a service and information economy, with reductions in "material intensity" and the introduction of clean and resource-efficient technologies. The emphasis is on global solutions to problems of environmental sustainability.
- *B2*: Solutions to problems of economic, social, and environmental sustainability are supposed to be local. The global population continues to increase, though at a lower rate than in *A2*. There is more diverse technological change than in *B1* or *A1*. Economic growth is intermediate. The critical difference from *B1*, besides the assumption of population growth, is that environmental solutions are local rather than global.

It was not possible for the IPCC to assign credible probabilities to the scenarios, and that task remains impossible today, as does such an assignment to individual scenarios within each family. Of 40 scenarios that it analyzed, the IPPCC selected six for special attention. One came from each of the *A2*, *B1*, and *B2* families, and three came from *A1*: *A1FI*, technology would be fossil fuel-intensive; *A1B*, there would be a balance between fossil fuels and alternative energy; and *A1T*, there would be a transition to predominantly alternative energy technologies.

For these six scenarios, the IPCC projected fossil fuel emissions in 2100 as follows, quantifying all emissions of greenhouse gases as if they were emissions of carbon dioxide in the effect they produce on temperature increase: *B1*, 600 ppmv; *A1T*, 700 ppmv; *B2*, 800 ppmv; *A1B*, 850 ppmv; *A2*, 1250 ppmv; and *A1FI*, 1550 ppmv. *B1* and *A1FI* are the most extreme. These computations already involve the use of models and the IPCC made no effort to deny the uncertainties associated with these models. But the results remain plausible to any informed and unbiased observer (including the legions of scientific experts who review the IPCC's work). The point is that we still must act in the presence of such uncertainties, and our best scientific consensus is all we can rely on, given the absence of an oracle to consult.

Most subsequent uses of these scenarios have ignored *A1FI* (including the 2007 IPCC assessment), presumably because there is already sufficient political will to reduce emissions to make that scenario irrelevant. Instead, they have considered the other five, or taken three to be representative (usually, *B1*, *A1B*, and *A2* as, for instance, in the 2007 IPCC assessment), or just the two extremes; that is, *B1* and *A2*. The first two of these strategies constitute robustness analysis; the third constitutes an extremal model analysis (see Table 4.2).

The next stage is the construction of models for each scenario. Now, there are two important choices: what should be included in a model, and how should the factors that are included be modeled? We will ignore the second issue here since it is inherently technical, though different choices should again be subject to the type of uncertainty analysis described in Table 4.2. Turning to the first issue, there is a hierarchy of models that are available, and this description is intended to be illustrative rather than exhaustive:

(1) There are global models that uniformly cover the entire Earth. However, these can be computed at a reasonable spatial resolution only if we include very few of the processes known to be relevant to climate change (because of limitations in terms of both speed of computation and required computer memory). We gain *generality* at the expense of *detail* in prediction and with respect to what processes can be included.

(2) Suppose we give up a bit on resolution but include more processes. We end up with Earth-system Models of Intermediate Complexity (EMICs). These are often a useful check on models that try to include much more detail.

73

(3) The most important are regional models embedded in a General Circulation Model (GCM). These can include both atmospheric and oceanic circulation. When both are included we have coupled Atmosphere Ocean General Circulation Models (AOGCMs). We get finer resolution than with the global models and EMIC but we have to worry whether putting together regional models in this way is epistemologically justified.

(4) Finally, there are the Regional Climate Models (RCMs) themselves, which can be computed at finer resolutions—and the level of detail that can be obtained depends on the resolution—but, obviously, we lose generality. These models can include mechanisms such as carbon cycles more credibly than AOGCMs, though with increasing computational power that constraint is rapidly disappearing.

By and large, the 2007 IPCC assessment relies on AOGCMs, using 23 different models to investigate mainly the *B1*, *A1B*, and *A2* scenarios, though some of the analyses included all six canonical scenarios. Taking model uncertainties into account by averaging over all the models for a given scenario, the IPCC's projections on temperature increase are: *B1*, 1.8 °C (1.1–2.9 °C); *B2*, 2.4 °C (1.4–3.8 °C); *A1B*, 2.8 °C (1.7–4.4 °C); *A1T*, 2.4 °C (1.4–3.8 °C); *A2*, 3.4 °C (2.0–5.4 °C); and *A1FI*, 4.0 °C (2.4–6.4 °C). Uncertainty is quantitatively reported by indicating the range of predicted temperature increases. There is ample reason for worry about the extent of likely warming. In the worst-case scenario, what previously took nearly 20 000 years could be replicated in a century. It should also not go unnoticed that the order of the scenarios on the basis of predicted temperature increases is not the same as the order on the basis of the predicted emissions under each scenario: *A1B*, *A1T*, and *B2* do not appear in the same order.

This example is important because climate change has come to be credibly perceived as one of the most important environmental problems of our time.

When dealing with complex environmental contexts, all models involved in the assessment stages of Table 4.1 will suffer from such uncertainties. What should we make of such uncertainties? Two questions should be separated. (1) What should we believe, given the model uncertainties? (2) How should we act in the face of these uncertainties? Both questions are of obvious philosophical interest. The second has received ample attention and will be taken up in the next section. The methods described in that section assume that uncertainties can be quantified as probabilities. However, that requires, at the very least, that we answer the first question.[6] Table 4.2 lists some of the approaches used to address the first question and the quite severe epistemological problems associated with them. None of these strategies leads to particularly credible results and further epistemological work on developing more reliable methods would not go unnoticed.

Table 4.2 Coping with Model Uncertainty

Model averaging	One strategy endorsed, for instance, by the governmental United States Climate Change Science Program is to use averages across the results from all available models. What makes this strategy attractive is that it can be carried out quite easily in practice. However, it assumes that the results predicted by available models form a representative sample. This means that they must span all results from the range of feasible (physically allowable) models and the frequency of each type of model must equal its probability of being correct. These are impossible criteria to verify in practice. Model averaging as a strategy of addressing model uncertainty has few epistemological virtues beyond the fact that it can be carried out in practice.
Robustness analysis	Model results are supposed to be reliable if they are predicted by all (available) models (which, typically, make important incompatible assumptions). In ecology this principle was first proposed in the 1960s by Richard

75

Table 4.2 (*Continued*)

	Levins, who coined the beguiling slogan: "Truth is the intersection of independent lies."[7] Within the philosophy of science the principle has been vigorously promoted by figures such as Bill Wimsatt.[8] However, establishing its rigorous basis using either logical or probabilistic reasoning has proved elusive (as Elliott Sober and others have pointed out).[9] Now, if the results from the available models fully span the range of results from all feasible models, obviously we should have somewhat more confidence in the results. (It does not matter in the least whether the available models make incompatible assumptions, though, to some extent, they must: otherwise they would not be different models.) Beyond that, though, it is hard to see what additional reliability this type of robustness analysis provides. Nevertheless, it remains an intriguing suggestion. In practice, it is typically impossible to ensure that all feasible models have been considered, or at least properly sampled. An additional problem with robustness analysis is that it treats every model on par with every other, which ignores that fact that some models may have a much lower probability of being correct than others. Under robustness analysis, for a conclusion to be accepted, it must concur even with a very unlikely model.
Extremal models	Results are deemed reliable if they follow from extremal models; that is, models with the most extreme predictions in each direction. Alternatively, we could use those models that make the most extreme assumptions. For instance, in the case of climate change models, if we thought that temperature was the most important predicted primary result, we could use the scenarios from *A2* and *B1* families (see Box 4.1, ignoring the *A1FI* scenario because of its extreme implausibility) and privilege those results that are common to models of both these scenarios. Essentially this strategy is a simplified form of robustness analysis (described

Table 4.2 *(Continued)*

above). It is reliable only if all feasible non-extremal models produce (secondary) results that fall within the range demarcated by the results from the extremal models. The problems noted above in the case of robustness analysis resurface with a vengeance. In particular, it may well be the case that extremal models are highly unlikely and their use may severely limit what should be concluded in a given circumstance. In Box 4.1 there is no monotonic relationship between emissions and temperature change due to climate change (as predicted by the models: look at the *A1B*, *A1T*, and *B2* scenarios; however these are not the extremal models).

In many contexts, we are faced with an even worse epistemological prospect, one in which either (1) methods of the sort discussed in Table 4.1 do not yield unequivocal results or (2) the uncertainties cannot be credibly quantitatively assessed. For some, the uncertainties associated with future climate change are uncertainties of this sort—note how Box 4.1 *projects* rather than *predicts* future emission scenarios and temperature changes. In response, in recent years, many environmentalists and policy analysts have advocated the use of a *precautionary* approach in such contexts, employing a "precautionary principle" that has proved controversial—see Box 4.2 for detail. The idea is that some envi-

Box 4.2   The Precautionary Principle

Though it embodies the traditional folk wisdom that "it is better to be safe than sorry," which goes back centuries, the precautionary principle (PP) was first explicitly articulated in Germany as the *Vorsorgeprinzip* (literally, "foresight principle") in the 1970s as a way of responding to environmental risks.[10] The PP has been incorporated into several international treaties and declarations and has been extensively used. European countries have used the PP to ban UK beef (because of mad cow disease) and GM food, and even to minimize public exposure to electromagnetic radiation.

There have been many formulations of the PP, none canonical.[11] In this discussion, we will use versions that have had some policy relevance at the international level. Consider two such versions. In 1992, the United Nations formulated the PP as follows:

> In order to protect the environment, the precautionary principle shall be widely applied by States according to their capabilities. Where there are threats of serious or irreversible damage, lack of full scientific certainty shall not be used as a reason for postponing cost-effective measures to prevent environmental degradation.[12]

Over a decade later (in 2005), an expert group convened by the United Nations Educational, Scientific and Cultural Organization (UNESCO) formulated a variant: "When human activities may lead to morally unacceptable harm that is scientifically plausible but uncertain, actions shall be taken to avoid or diminish that harm."[13] *Morally unacceptable* harm was defined as that threatening to human life or health, or serious and effectively irreversible, or inequitable for present or future generations, or imposed without adequate consideration of the human rights of those affected. *Plausibility* was supposed to be grounded on scientific analysis (see below for further discussion). Further, *uncertainty* was supposed to "apply to, but [perhaps] not be limited to, causality of the bounds of possible harm," presumably meaning that the relevant probabilities cannot be accurately assessed. Meanwhile, the PP generated fierce criticism for being a conservative risk-averse rule that would stifle scientific progress, change, and growth, with one critic labeling it as "the application of junk science to phantom risks to make them seem plausible."[14]

Both the UN and UNESCO definitions essentially agree that the PP should only be invoked if there is potential for significant (serious) harm, though the UNESCO version muddies the discussion by introducing a somewhat wild disjunction of heterogeneous factors. The UN definition has the advantage of requiring action only if cost-effective options are available—if they are not, it is hard to see how the PP can credibly guide policy choices. Conversely, the UNESCO definition has the advantage of requiring the potential harm to be plausible—if such a constraint is not put on the applicability of the PP it would preclude policy options in the face of miniscule risks; for instance, of a fatal accident every time we use a vehicle.

In defense of the PP, Resnik and others have urged the incorporation of both criteria—the plausibility of the serious harm and the availability of reasonable responses—into the definition of the PP.[15] Requiring the availability of a reasonable response, and being able to decide when a response is reasonable, does not place any undue burden on potential PP users. The question that remains is whether the criterion of plausibility can itself be plausibly formulated. It cannot reduce to some required level of probability—otherwise we could use standard risk analysis in decision theory.[16] Given that plausibility has to be based on scientific analyses, Resnik offers the following six criteria (which were subsequently endorsed in the UNESCO report) for the plausibility of a hypothesis:

(1) *Coherence*: The hypothesis should be consistent with background knowledge and theories.
(2) *Explanatory power*: The hypothesis should be able to explain important phenomena.

(3) *Analogy*: the hypothesis should posit casual mechanisms similar to well-understood ones.

(4) *Precedence*: Events posited by the hypotheses should be similar to previously observed ones.

(5) *Precision*: The hypothesis should be reasonably precise.

(6) *Simplicity*: Simpler hypotheses are better than more complex ones.

These criteria are neither meant to be necessary nor sufficient. They are essentially heuristic rules that Resnik has borrowed from the philosophy of science, where they are used as subsidiary rules for theory acceptance when more than one theory is empirically adequate (in the sense of predicting the results of experiments correctly).

It is far from obvious that these rules can effectively be used in practice to adjudicate environmental (or other) disputes. They may simply not be precise enough (and they have never been convincingly formalized in the philosophy of science for the purpose of theory acceptance). If the rules cannot be used in practice, it may well make more sense to advocate a precautionary approach rather than invoke a PP. Having to resort to the PP may only signify that we need to return to a deliberative mode of decision making, and to realize that formal analysis is of no further help.

ronmental problems such as climate change are so serious that we need to act even when standard decision theory (including risk analysis) provides no answer.

Decision Theory

How should we put science and ethics together, especially in the face of uncertainty? What is called decision theory attempts to provide a set of systematic methods to achieve this goal. When it is informal, it provides guidelines for ensuring that ethical issues are explicitly discussed during environmental decisions. When it is formal, it develops explicit protocols ("decision protocols" or "decision-theoretic protocols") that use a set of logical and mathematical techniques to evaluate and rank alternatives (policy options). What makes formal decision theory important and attractive in many policy-making contexts is that its use ensures explicitness and repeatability: all the factors that went into a decision must be laid out explicitly, and, when the decision analysis is repeated, the same result will be reached. We will focus on formal decision theory because the informal versions are typically no more than verbal implementations of formal methods that must be used because of insufficient or insufficiently precise data (see below). As this section will show, decision theory raises a host of epistemological issues besides troubling questions about the nature of rational choice. There are few areas of contemporary philosophy that are equally interesting.

Decision theory emerged in the twentieth century when philosophers such as Frank Ramsey attempted to give a precise characterization of rational choice in the presence of uncertainty using the tools of probability theory. Many of the most important contributions have come from economists. Rationality serves as a normative goal in decision analyses, specifying how agents *should* behave under the circumstances. Consequently, decision analysis is a normative enterprise. As we shall see, the normative aspect of decision analysis has important philosophical consequences. (Descriptive decision analysis to describe how people make decisions in practice also exists: it will be ignored here since it is not relevant to our context.)

Decisions are made by single *agents* or *groups* of agents. Individuals making decisions are typical agents. Potentially, a composite unit such as a corporation making a decision can also be modeled as a single agent. Exactly when a composite body of individuals may plausibly be treated as a single agent is an interesting question that has so far not received a convincing precise answer: philosophically, one would say that it is a situation when the whole has an identity of its own that is, in some sense, independent of its parts. In practice, the following criterion seems reasonable: if the composite body as a whole has a clearly articulated and individuated goal, then it may be treated as a single agent. For instance, a composite body with the goal of reducing water pollution to a specified level has such a goal. One that wants to protect nature in some region probably does not: as we saw in Chapter 2, there is a wide array of natural values that may be in conflict with each other. Consequently, without further analysis, the goal of such a body is not adequately individuated: different members of the group may be pursuing conflicting goals.

After the specification of a goal, decision analysis assumes that there is a set of *alternatives* (for instance, environmental policies) that must be ranked by the agent(s). Most formal methods assume that this set of alternatives is fixed at the outset and this discussion will be restricted to that context. This is a strong assumption: in many decision contexts, the most difficult part may well be to become clear on the goal and to identify the set of alternatives.[17] Next, the alternatives must be evaluated by some *criteria* in order to decide between them. We will initially restrict attention to decisions using a single criterion—most of the interesting philosophical problems have arisen in this context. Decisions with multiple criteria will be discussed later in this section.

At the very least, each criterion must rank all the alternatives: given any two alternatives, one must be better than, worse than, or as good as the other. (More formally, each criterion must impose a weak total order on the alternative set, *total* because every pair of alternatives is ranked and *weak* because two alternatives can be as good as each other.) Such a ranking is called *ordinal*. Without this minimal assumption about criteria, it is impossible to use a criterion to evaluate the alternatives: because of that, this assumption is usually taken to be uncontroversial. A stronger assumption requires that each alternative is attributed a definite quantitative performance measure by the criterion, and such a ranking is called *quantitative*. A quantitative ranking is stronger than an ordinal ranking because the quantitative measures naturally induce an order among the alternatives but we can have such an order without quantitative measures. However, two different quantitative rankings (*e.g.*, $A = 1$,

$B = 4$, $C = 5$ and $A = 1$, $B = 2$, $C = 5$) may produce the same ordinal ranking (in this example $<A, B, C>$).

Whether we should only assume ordinal rankings or quantitative ones depends on the alternatives and the criterion. Suppose, for instance, that the alternatives are various designs for a city park. Suppose that we use shape as the criterion by which we want to sort alternatives. It seems reasonable to suppose that we can ordinally rank various proposed park configurations by their shape but not plausible to associate a numerical measure with shape. In contrast, suppose that our criterion is the cost of the land: it is now entirely plausible to use quantitative performance measures.

So far we have assumed that there is no uncertainty about selecting an alternative in the sense that, if we decide on an alternative (which is a potential environmental policy), that is the one that will be implemented. If a ranking is ordinal, presumably any rational agent should select the alternative(s) with the highest rank(s); similarly, if a ranking is quantitative, the same agent should select the alternative (s) with the highest performance measure(s). It may be the case that there are ties between alternatives: but, in that case, formal decision analysis can go no further and the decision maker is left to deliberate more on whether there is any ground for preferring one alternative over another.

A much more interesting situation arises when there is uncertainty. We will assume the simplest case: there is a probability associated with each alternative that expresses how likely it is to be realized. If the alternatives only have an ordinal ranking by the criteria, there is little that decision analysis can do and we will ignore that case, though it is quite likely to be encountered in practice. (Return to the city park example and suppose that we have to worry about whether each configuration is politically feasible, and we represent this uncertainty using probabilities.) If the alternatives have a quantitative ranking, we encounter some even more troubling philosophical problems.

Economists assume that the performance measures of the alternatives reflect an agent's *value* function: how that agent should (internally) value each alternative. If we multiply this value with the probability of that alternative, we obtain the agent's *expected value* or *utility* for that alternative. Once we have the utilities for all the alternatives, we have the agent's utility function. (Note that what is being called "value" here is sometimes called "utility" in the literature; in that terminology, our "utility" becomes "expected utility." The choice here reflects standard usage in multi-criteria decision analysis.) Now we get the central normative principle for making decisions: a rational agent should act to maximize this utility function.[18]

Problems abound: (1) The most serious of these is simply stated: what are these utility functions? They are obviously theoretical constructs: abstract entities somehow related to agents' felt preferences. At first glance, we may want to say that they serve the same role in economics as atoms or fields do in physics or valency does in chemistry. Unfortunately, this analogy does not work. Theoretical entities in the (descriptive) natural sciences receive their support from their ability to describe the behavior of systems (typically through predicted experimental results). If that test were used for utility theory, it would fail miserably: people often do not behave as if they were maximizing their utility functions. However, this is an unfair criticism: decision analysis is a normative enterprise and not a descriptive one. It is supposed to capture how people should behave, not necessarily how they do behave. But, then, what is the justification for any theory used in decision analysis? The response has been to begin with some assumptions about rational behavior that appear to be uncontroversial to everyone (we will see some of these in Box 4.3). We then attempt to show that the principles of this theory are logically entailed by these assumptions. For utility theory such a justification was provided by von Neumann and Morgenstern in their pioneering work on game theory in the 1940s.[19] The trouble is, though, that their normative assumptions, however plausible, generate many paradoxes.

(2) In other words, is it even clear that we should (normatively) try to maximize our utility? Consider a case in which the value of alternatives is measured by the number of species that can be protected in a conservation area. Assume that alternative *A* has value of 2 on this measure (for instance, two species can be pro-

tected), and that *B* has value 2000. However, the probability of successfully implementing *A* is 0.9 whereas that for *B* is 0.001. This means the utility of *A* is 1.8 and that of *B* is 2.0. *B* is preferred to *A* but it is far from clear that it is rational to choose an alternative with such a low probability in this case. There are many other (more troubling, but more complicated) odd consequences of utility theory and these have been extensively analyzed by philosophers.[20]

Other complications arise when we include the cases in which decisions involve groups (multiple agents), multiple criteria, or both.

(a) *Group decisions:*[21] Environmental decisions are often made by groups; when these are political decisions, this is almost always the case. This process requires the aggregation of rankings produced by the individuals of a group. There exist a bewildering variety of methods for aggregation. Voting is one such method: its rationality is relatively easy to defend in simple situations; for instance, when there are only two alternatives and all members of the group have equal status. However, even with voting there are potential problems. For instance, suppose that there are three members in a group and two of them rank one alternative, *A*, over the alternative, *B*, whereas the third ranks *B* over *A*. Voting would result in a group ranking of *A* over *B*. However, suppose that the first two individuals only have a very slight preference of *A* over *B* whereas the third very strongly prefers *B* over *A*. In using simple voting, have we compounded the individual ranks (or preferences) rationally? More generally, if we assume that alternatives are being evaluated on a quantitative scale using value or utility functions, we need to aggregate these and we are faced with the problem of comparing interpersonal preferences. Individuals *i* and *j* may both think that alternative *A* is three times better than alternative *B* by some criterion; yet *i* feels that the criterion in question is of no great import but *j* feels it is crucial. How are we to aggregate their value/utility functions rationally? There is no obvious solution. And there is worse to come. As was noted earlier, the methods of decision theory are supposed to receive their warrant from being entailed by uncontroversial assumptions about rationality. For group decisions, Kenneth Arrow managed to show that there can be no procedure that satisfies four apparently trivial and non-controversial assumptions about group decisions (see Box 4.3 for a more detailed discussion of this point).[23]

Box 4.3   Arrow's Theorem[22]

Suppose that there is a group, G, of decision makers who have to rank alternatives belonging to a set A. Members of G will be designated g_1, g_2, *etc.*; those of A, a_1, a_2, *etc.* Each member of the group, G, will be presumed to have an ordinal ranking of all members of A; that is, of all the alternatives. The purpose of a group decision procedure, P, is to produce a group ranking of the members of A based on these individual rankings. Let us impose four apparently uncontroversial minimal conditions that any rational group ranking procedure should satisfy:

- *Unrestricted scope/collective rationality*: P should be able to handle any set of internally coherent rankings of A produced by members of G.
- *Dominance*: If every member of G ranks a_i higher than a_j, then P must rank a_i higher than a_j.
- *Non-dictatorship*: P cannot take the ranking of any single individual, g^*, and automatically make it the group ranking. (Otherwise g^* would be a dictator.)
- *Independence of irrelevant alternatives*: The group ranking of a given set of alternatives should only depend on how the individuals rank those alternatives, and not at all on how they rank other alternatives.

Arrow showed that there is no P that can satisfy all four of these conditions.

Philosophers have been debating the meaning of Arrow's theorem since it was published in 1951. Since each of the conditions discussed above seems inherently rational, one possible conclusion may be that it is simply impossible to design a rational group decision procedure. Alternatively, we could try to show that, initial impressions to the contrary, at least one of the four assumptions does not capture an uncontroversial aspect of rationality. Many commentators question the fourth assumption, which says that how one should rank a given set of alternatives should not depend on what other alternatives are around. However, if we think that rankings depend on the global context of what alternatives are available, then this assumption would not be warranted.

(b) *Multiple criteria*: Some of the same problems persist when we turn to multi-criteria decisions, and some new ones emerge. Note that multi-criteria analysis is unavoidable in almost all environmental decision scenarios. Almost every environmentally desirable criterion must compete with economic cost (another criterion) and tradeoffs must be introduced between them. Most scenarios are much more complex. Take the design of urban parks: criteria will include shape, size, vegetation type, public accessibility, acquisition cost, maintenance cost, *etc.* In what follows we assume that there are multiple criteria and one agent. (Extension of the discussion to multi-criteria multi-agent situations is straightforward.[24]) If the criteria themselves have no order, there is only one straightforward rational strategy: the selection of all non-dominated alternatives. An alternative dominates another if the first is better than the second by at least one criterion and no worse than the second by any criterion. Non-dominated alternatives are those that are not dominated by any other alternatives. If there is only one non-dominated alternative, it is clearly the best decision. However, typically, the number of non-dominated alternatives increases with the number of criteria (see the example in Box 4.4). Consequently, additional methods must be used to sort these non-dominated alternatives. A wide variety of methods for multi-criteria analysis (MCA) have been proposed over the years; unfortunately, most of these have no foundation in accounts of

Box 4.4   Multi-Criteria Decision Analysis in
Northeastern Namibia

Figure 4.1 shows an area of northern Namibia, in southern
Africa. The region in dark gray is the Etosha National Park,
one of the world's premier wildlife reserves.[26] Community
planners from the region north of Etosha envisioned setting
aside some of the land parcels for the conservation of biodiversity while accommodating perceived social needs and
aspirations.

There were 120 land parcels: cells of varying sizes and
shapes determined by political administrative boundaries.
Thirty-five vegetation types found in the region were used as
biodiversity surrogates (for more discussion of the selection
of such surrogates, see Chapter 5). The biodiversity representation target was to put under protective management 10
percent of each vegetation type, including what is present in
Etosha, besides the additional land parcels that were being
selected for this purpose. Human needs and aspirations were
modeled using six criteria: (1) the total area that must be set
aside for protection; (2) the total human population that
would be affected; (3) the number of winter cattle; (4) the
number of summer cattle; (5) the farming potential of a cell;
and (6) the number of wildlife present. The first five of these
criteria were supposed to be minimized while the last is
supposed to be maximized. The numbers of summer and
winter cattle can be very different because of local grazing
practices and thus must be considered separately. The number of wildlife is a social criterion in this context because it is
supposed to measure the ecotourism potential of an area.

Planning began with the identification of one hundred
alternative plans, each of which consisted of a set of selected
cells, including Etosha, that represented the vegetation types
at or above the 10 percent representation target. Each unique

alternative was ranked, initially ordinally, according to each of the six socio-economic criteria. Then, the non-dominated alternatives were computed. There were 24 non-dominated alternatives.

Had the number of non-dominated alternatives been small (typically, less than 10), these would have been handed over to the political decision-makers for further refinement via deliberation. However, 24 is probably far too many alternatives to hand over in this way, and further decision analysis must be used to narrow down the set of remaining alternatives further. As explained in the text, such attempts require more controversial assumptions. First, all alternatives must be ranked quantitatively according to each criterion; that is, a definite quantitative value must be set for them. This is relatively straightforward in this case because the data consist of such numerical measurements. Second, the criteria must be cardinally ranked on a quantitative scale. In this case, pairwise preference comparisons were elicited from the stakeholders and aggregated: for each pair of criteria, the stakeholders were asked to specify how many times one was better than the other. (Note that the stakeholders were being treated as a single agent.) The responses were checked for consistency and then the results were aggregated using multi-attribute value theory. To ensure that a linear value function was appropriate, each pair of criteria were checked for difference independence. Two examples will suffice: (1) clearly the value of a change in the number of winter cattle did not depend on how many summer cattle there were and *vice versa* and (2) similarly, within the possible range of human population change in that region, the value of a change in the human population did not depend on the number of wildlife present. There were 15 such comparisons that had to be analyzed. Figure 4.1(a) and Figure 4.1(b) are the two plans that were ranked highest. Note that the differences are minor.

(a)

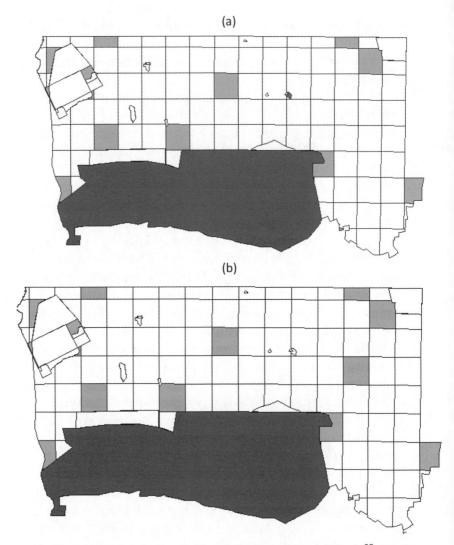

(b)

Figure 4.1 Selected areas north of Etosha National Park.[25] Etosha National Park is shown in dark gray; the selected areas in light gray; (a) shows a tiny parcel of land in the north east that is replaced by a larger, square parcel in (b).

agents' preferences and, therefore, have no rational basis.[27] However, multi-attribute utility (and value) theory has been developed as a generalization of (single-criterion) utility theory, mentioned earlier.[28] The use of this theory requires that each alternative be attributed a quantitative value by each criterion and that the criteria themselves have quantitative weights associated with them. Moreover, some subtle independence conditions between the criteria must also be satisfied. For instance, the existence of a unique value function requires *difference independence* between each pair of criteria: the difference in the value function induced by a specified change according to one criterion must not depend on the performance of the alternative according to the other criterion. An illustration will show how easily this criterion may be violated. Suppose, as before, we are designing urban parks. If proposed parks (the alternatives) are tiny in size, we may be very bothered by a minor difference of shape; if the parks are rather large, we may not care at all about such a small shape change. Difference independence is thus violated. Box 4.4 gives an example of the use of multi-attribute value theory. Finally, multi-criteria decisions also suffer from the problems raised by Arrow's theorem. The reason for this is that there is a straightforward isomorphism (identity of mathematical structure) between the structure of group decisions and that of multi-criteria decisions: in the former we have one criteria and multiple agents, in the latter we have one agent and multiple criteria, and the logic of aggregation is the same in both cases.[29]

The philosophical problems that have been discussed in this section are associated with decision analysis in general, and not special problems encountered in environmental contexts. However, because environmental decision makers are increasingly beginning to use decision theory as a tool, they would do well to be aware of these problems. For instance, the problems with group decision procedures may convince them to try to reach consensus between members of a group through deliberation rather than to use any formal procedure. Similarly, for multi-criteria decisions, they may spend some time to make sure that the criteria used will have suitably independent measures.

Environmental decision contexts do, however, pose a severe problem also seen in some (but not most other) contexts: not only must we act under remarkable uncertainty but we must do so under severe time constraints, and the results of decisions will often be completely irreversible. Consider an example. A town is deciding which of two adjacent areas will be conserved for natural values and which will be converted into an industrial complex. Assuming that the relevant natural values include biodiversity, we may want to make inventories of the two areas for the biota they contain. But such surveys take time and cost money and the town's governing body wants a decision within months because of pressures from potential developers. And, once the decision is made, the land that is transformed will in most cases never regain its original state; if it contained endemic species, they will probably become extinct. This is not an artificial example concocted to illustrate a philosophical point: for example, in central Texas we routinely face this issue because the land under us often consists of karst fissures containing an unknown number of endemic unstudied invertebrates.

Who Is a Legitimate Stakeholder?

In the discussion of group decisions, earlier, it was assumed that there is a set of appropriate stakeholders whose preferences have to be accommodated. Stakeholder involvement in environmental decisions has emerged as a standard and very politically correct aspect of environmental decisions during the last two decades, even in relatively remote areas of the Earth. Stakeholder involvement was introduced in response to criticisms that national and transnational environmental organizations, especially those promoting the conservation of wildlife (such as national wildlife NGOs and the WWF) were imposing management policies on habitats without taking into account the interests or basic human rights of those who lived on them. (Recall Box 1.1.) In response, WWF and other transnational environmental NGOs began to claim that they were committed to the welfare of local residents and would encourage local participation in management decisions. In Asia, even the International Centre for Integrated Mountain Development (ICIMOD), a huge government-sponsored organization involving eight Himalayan countries, identifies "local people" besides government as stakeholders in development and biodiversity conservation decisions.[30]

Nevertheless, Mark Dowie and other critics have pointed out that it is questionable whether these commitments from NGOs and other such organizations are anything more than window-dressing designed to deflect attention from serious ethical problems.[31] Two types of ethical problem merit particular attention.

The first has analogs elsewhere, particularly biomedical ethics. Let us begin with a standard distinction, between "top-down" and "bottom-up" modes of decision making. The former consists of external authorities higher in power hierarchies making decisions for local agents—and, in the most extreme forms, imposing them on these agents. One well-known extreme example is that of national governments creating protected areas such as national parks and implementing them by forcible eviction of local residents. The latter mode consists of decisions made by local agents and then co-ordinated, to the extent necessary, with those higher in power hierarchies.

Consider circumstances in which stakeholders include both designated representatives of remote governments and local residents. In most situations (with ICIMOD providing a typical example) most parameters of the decision scenario—for instance, the delineation of feasible alternatives and even the relevant criteria—are set by the non-local stakeholders, reinforcing the asymmetries of power in such negotiations. In situations such as these, it is far from clear that the voices of all stakeholders receive adequate representation, even when all of them are included as co-participants. The situation is made worse by the fact that local stakeholders will often have an inadequate understanding of the issues involved—for instance, the assumptions made by models invoked by the non-local stakeholders—or of how to interpret the various uncertainties involved (even if these are explicitly brought to the table). Besides the asymmetries of power, there are asymmetries of knowledge. In other words, the decision-making process remains top-down even though it pretends to be at least partly bottom-up by including local stakeholders. The analog here is with informed consent in biomedical contexts.

The second problem is that of delineating the stakeholders themselves. Who is a legitimate stakeholder? Who decides? Consider a well-known example from the 1990s: the struggle of local groups against transnational oil companies extracting petroleum in the Niger Delta of Nigeria.[32] A transnational corporation, Shell, backed by a vicious and corrupt military dictatorship, was confronted by a local organization, the Movement for the Survival of the Ogoni People (MOSOP), which demanded increased local autonomy, a fair share of profits, and remediation of health-threatening pollution from oil extraction. (What shocked the world and made this example famous was the execution of nine MOSOP leaders on trumped-up charges in 1995 without any semblance of a fair trial; those murdered included the internationally prominent Nigerian author, Ken Saro-Wiwa.) Now, suppose that this dispute was to be resolved using stakeholder negotiations. Few would doubt that the local people (represented either by MOSOP or in some other acceptable way) were legitimate stakeholders. But what about the military dictatorship then governing Nigeria? Even if we concede that national governments are always legitimate stakeholders—and this is open to dispute—is a military dictatorship ever a legitimate stakeholder? What about Shell? Does the fact that it had made an economic investment in the Niger delta automatically give it a legitimate seat at the table? Stakeholder legitimacy is a politically (and ethically) debatable question of obvious philosophical importance. So far it has never received the kind of philosophical attention it merits. The place to start may well be in the legal arena: for instance, in the United States, by analyzing how courts decide who has legal standing in a case. However, identifying legitimate stakeholders involves more than legal reasoning—we should not abrogate our deeper ethical responsibilities, which go beyond what is appropriate in a legal context.

Notes

1. Such a deployment should be central to Minteer and Collins' (2008) somewhat controversial project of "ecological ethics" though they seem to eschew formal analysis. Their project is only controversial insofar as it is based on an assumption that environmental ethics is overwhelmingly committed to non-anthropocentrism; if that were true, it is hard to see why McShane (2007), for instance, has to exhort environmental ethicists not to abandon intrinsic value attributions (which are central to non-anthropocentrism—recall the discussion of Chapter 3). However, the discussions of this chapter embrace one of the central goals of ecological ethics: the translation of values into practical policies taking empirical knowledge into account.
2. Resnik (1987) provides a useful introduction to philosophical problems and paradoxes of decision theory.
3. Other problems and developments will largely be identified in footnotes that direct attention to the relevant literature.
4. For a different view of the relation between models and theories, see van Fraassen (1980).
5. For the IPCC emission scenarios, see Intergovernmental Panel on Climate Change (2000). The projections reported here are from Meehl *et al.* (2007).
6. At the very least, we may need to assign a "degree of belief" between 0 and 1 to the consequences of our decisions.
7. See Levins (1966), p. 423.
8. See Wimsatt (1980).
9. See Orzack and Sober (1993); for responses, see Levins (1993) and Odenbaugh (2003).
10. See Resnik (2003) and COMEST (2005); the latter source also cites a possible Swedish origin.
11. Stirling (2007) provides 19 versions.
12. UN (1992), p. 10, as quoted by Resnik (2003), p. 330.
13. COMEST (2005), p. 14.
14. Hugh Wise, from the US Environmental Protection Agency's Office of Water, as quoted in Resnik (2003), p. 330.
15. See Resnik (2003); for a different defense, see Stirling (2007). Peterson (2006) argues for the incoherence of the PP after interpreting it as a

     different decision rule from the one analyzed in the text (which was motivated by the usage adopted by most agencies that defend the PP).

16. Resnik (2003, p. 341) gives the following example: "Thus, if I spot a new growth on my skin and my two hypotheses are 'it's cancerous' and 'it's benign,' I do not have to determine that the growth is probably cancerous in order to go to the doctor and have it tested."

17. For extensive philosophical elaborations of this point, see Levi (1986) and Morton (1991).

18. A particularly simple (in mathematical parlance, "degenerate") form of expected utility analysis is cost-benefit analysis, which has been extensively used in environmental decision making though it is gradually being replaced by the more sophisticated methods discussed in the text. In cost-benefit analysis, we imagine that the expected utility of an action can be evaluated as the difference between its (expected) benefit and its (expected) cost. If the benefits outweigh the cost, we are supposed to endorse the action. In most contexts of the use of cost-benefit analysis, the costs and benefits are interpreted in economic terms. For lack of space we will eschew further discussion of cost-benefit analysis—see Norton (1987) for a critical discussion in the context of the conservation of species.

19. See von Neumann and Morgenstern (1944).

20. Note that maximizing utilities is not the only possible decision rule—see Resnik (1987) for a discussion of others such as *maximin* (choose the alternative with the highest worst outcome) or *maximax* (choose the alternative with the highest best outcome). These are being ignored here for lack of space.

21. Group decisions can also be analyzed using game theory, especially in circumstances in which members of the group are responding to each other's decisions. These models will be ignored here for lack of space—see Frank and Sarkar (2010) for an example of using game theory in the context of biodiversity conservation decisions.

22. The discussion is simplified from MacKay (1980).

23. See Arrow (1950, 1963). MacKay (1980) provides a good philosophical discussion.

24. Doing so raises no new conceptual questions and, for that reason, will not be pursued any further here.

25. Redrawn using data from Moffett *et al.* (2006).

26. The example is from Moffett *et al.* (2006).

27. See the review by Moffett and Sarkar (2006).
28. See Keeney and Raiffa (1993) for multi-attribute utility theory and Dyer and Sarin (1979) for multi-attribute value theory.
29. This point was first noted by Arrow and Raynaud (1986).
30. See Guangwei (2002).
31. See Dowie (2009).
32. For more detail, see Okonta and Douglas (2003).

5

Biodiversity and Conservation

We turn, finally, to some of the most general goals of contemporary environmental movements, no matter whether the immediate problems they confront concern resource limitation, pollution, or climate change. There are four broad goals: conservation, restoration, sustainability, and equity. The conservation of biodiversity occupies this chapter; subsequent chapters take up each of the other goals. The ethical basis for biodiversity conservation was discussed in Chapter 3. This chapter focuses on conceptual and epistemological issues.

Biodiversity conservation is the central goal of *conservation biology*, which, as an organized academic discipline, is of very recent vintage. It emerged in the mid-1980s, first in the United States and then elsewhere in the North, especially Australia.[1] The immediate context was the rapidly increasing destruction, post-World War II, of tropical rain forests and other habitats recognized as critical repositories of biological diversity because of the number of distinctive species and ecological communities present in them. The term "biodiversity" was only introduced in 1986 as a contraction for "biological diversity." Many commentators have analyzed the synergistic growth of the use of the term "biodiversity" and the growing popularity of conservation biology as a discipline. Conservation biologists, particularly in the United States, felt that they were creating a brave new science. While this claim has little factual support (nature conservation, includ-

Environmental Philosophy: From Theory to Practice, First Edition. Sahotra Sarkar.
© 2012 John Wiley & Sons Inc. Published 2012 by John Wiley & Sons Inc.

ing the conservation of large complements of species, has a long history), it led conservation biologists to theorize about "biodiversity" while largely ignoring earlier attempts by ecologists to formulate a quantitative measure of ecological diversity.[2] One consequence of this history is that the best way philosophers have been able to make sense of the concept of biodiversity (which remains problematic when scrutinized carefully, as this chapter will show) is to view it in the context of the emergence of conservation biology: biodiversity is simply the goal pursued by the practice of conservation biology.[3]

A wide variety of practices fall under the rubric of conservation biology, which is a hybrid discipline incorporating insights from many areas of biology relevant to the persistence of biota and, arguably, also insights from the social sciences and the humanities (see below). The most relevant area within biology is ecology, which studies the interactions of species and individuals with each other and with the physical environment. The main differences between conservation biology and ecology are that the former embraces many other disciplines (as noted earlier, and emphasized below) and is explicitly a goal-oriented discipline aiming to ensure the persistence of biodiversity into the indefinite future. As such, conservation biology has a relation to ecology similar to that of medicine to biology.[4] However, in recent years, given the perceived seriousness of environmental problems, many ecologists have begun to rethink their discipline as one that has a societal mission and is also goal-directed.[5]

There is widespread agreement that a necessary component of conservation is the selection and management of areas for the continued persistence of biota. *Systematic conservation planning* (see Table 5.1 for a detailed description), which focuses on this component, recognizes three distinct goals for the design of *conservation area networks*, which are sets of areas prioritized for management for biodiversity conservation:[9]

(1) One aim must be for the conservation area networks to include all of the biodiversity of a region. This is called the goal of *representation*. Its satisfaction depends on how *biodiversity*

Table 5.1   Stages of Systematic Conservation Planning
Systematic conservation planning is a structured multi-component stage-wise approach to identifying conservation areas and devising management policy, with feedback, revision, and reiteration, where needed, at any stage. Figure 5.1 shows how these stages interact with each other.[7] As discussed in the text, the general goals of systematic conservation planning, during the design of conservation area networks, are representation, persistence, and economy.

Stage	Description
Choose and delimit the planning region	Stakeholders must explicitly discuss the precise geographical boundaries of the planning region at the beginning of any planning exercise. Different stakeholders may have different preferences for the boundaries of the planning unit. (Thus the choice of the planning region interacts with the identity and views of the stakeholders. The boundaries of the planning region will typically have a strong influence on what types of data compilation and analysis may be feasible.)
Identify all stakeholders	Conservation plans have little chance of successful implementation if they do not manage to negotiate successfully the socio-political issues relevant to the planning region, incorporate constraints, and take advantage of opportunities. Prospects for successful implementation are enhanced if all the relevant agents participate in the planning process from the beginning. The stakeholders will also have a role in implementing and monitoring a conservation plan at later stages. Stakeholders include biological and other experts. Obviously, the delineation of a planning region depends on the expert stakeholders and the choice of the planning region influences who qualifies as experts and other stakeholders. Though it is often ignored in practice (see Box 5.1 for an example), as noted in Chapter 4, determining who is a legitimate stakeholder requires attention to normative issues.

Table 5.1 *(Continued)*

Stage	Description
Compile and assess data	Conservation planning requires both biological and socio-political data. Sufficient resources are typically not available to collect all the data that would be useful. Data collection, for instance through surveys, should be cost-efficient and focused on those parameters that are the most important. Increasingly, planning is becoming reliant on publicly available resources such as the Global Biodiversity Information Facility (GBIF) and remotely sensed data. What data are most relevant is determined by the study region and the planning goals and objectives.
Treat data and construct models as necessary	Almost all data have inbuilt spatial and other biases that have to be removed through statistical refinement and modeling. In many planning contexts, species' geographical distributions have to be modeled from sparse opportunistic records and modeled environmental data. An extensive methodology has been developed for this purpose.
Identify and evaluate biodiversity constituents and surrogates	Care must be taken to ensure that biodiversity is appropriately represented and quantified. First, appropriate constituents of biodiversity (see the "Constituents and Surrogates" section) must be selected by stakeholders to represent the most important components of the regional biota that deserve conservation attention. If full distributional information on the biodiversity constituents is not obtainable, as is typically the case, surrogates for them must be identified.
Set explicit biodiversity goals and targets	It is crucial to be explicit about what constitutes adequate biodiversity protection. Quantitative targets of representation must be set for all biodiversity surrogates. Spatial configuration and other goals must similarly be explicitly speci-

(continued)

101

Table 5.1 (*Continued*)

Stage	Description
	fied—these goals are typically imposed to enhance the persistence of biodiversity in a conservation area network.
Review existing conservation areas for performance with respect to targets *Prioritize additional areas for conservation management*	The existing protected areas, if there are any, must be analyzed to determine the extent to which they already satisfy the specified goals and targets. New areas must be prioritized so that the specified goals and targets may be met when these areas are included in an expanded conservation area network. The problem is one of constrained optimization (as discussed in the text below). This stage may involve only achieving representation targets or may also incorporate other criteria, both spatial and socio-political. If these other criteria are being incorporated, multi-criteria analysis becomes relevant.
Assess biodiversity constituent and selected area vulnerabilities	A selected area may itself be vulnerable, in which case there is usually a poor prognosis for all its biodiversity constituents. Such vulnerability can arise from socio-political factors (for instance, development threat), existing ecological factors, or global change factors (such as climate change). Alternatively, only some of the constituents in the area may be vulnerable because of the quality of the habitat. If those constituents require that area to meet the relevant goals and targets, then the area itself should be considered vulnerable. Assessing vulnerability is typically very difficult. This part of systematic conservation planning remains poorly developed.
Refine the network of selected areas	If vulnerable areas are not entirely irreplaceable, a good strategy is to exclude them from nominal conservation area networks and repeat the area prioritization process. The vulnerability analysis

Table 5.1   *(Continued)*

Stage	Description
	must then be performed again, and the entire cycle must be reiterated until all goals and targets are met in a "safe" set of potential conservation areas.
Carry out multi-criteria analysis	If not all relevant criteria were incorporated at the stage of prioritizing new areas, a multi-criteria analysis must be performed to ensure that these criteria are incorporated into the design. Typically, multi-criteria analysis is done by generating a large number of "solutions" or potential conservation area networks, each of which satisfies the criteria that were used for area prioritization. These solutions are now evaluated and ranked using the other criteria.
Implement conservation plan	A nominal conservation area network must be implemented by devising appropriate management plans and then ensuring that they are put into practice. Implementation plans must take relevant contextual issues into account. While scientific analyses contribute towards devising a plan, implementation is almost entirely a sociopolitical process.
Monitor network performance	Biodiversity conservation is not a one-off process of delineating conservation area networks that can then be left to persist on their own. Both human encroachments and natural changes can alter the conservation status of a delineated area. Global factors such as climate change also play a role. Consequently, conservation area network performance must be continually monitored, and the planning process must be periodically repeated as part of adaptive management. This is easy to say but has proved hard to achieve.

Box 5.1 A Conservation Plan for the Merauke Region of Indonesian New Guinea (Papua Province)[6]

In 2008, the global NGO Conservation International (CI) contracted with the MEDCO group (an Indonesian conglomerate) to devise a land use plan for a forestry concession obtained by the latter in the Merauke region of Papua Province in Indonesian New Guinea. The planning area was thus determined by the Indonesian government—it is unclear that there was any prior consultation between the government and local residents (which is obviously ethically problematic—recall the discussion of Chapter 4). The goal was to achieve biodiversity conservation, ecosystem function maintenance, sustainable development (through forestry production), and satisfaction of community interests through an integration of communal values. MEDCO made a commitment to conserve 40 percent of the area; that is, to exempt such an area from plantation farming, along with the village areas of the communities living with the concession. This was a significant commitment to the conservation of biodiversity. The decision problem to be solved was where to situate that 40 percent.

The planning process began with a meeting between (among others) MEDCO and CI representatives in the presence of technical consultants (from the Biodiversity and Biocultural Conservation Laboratory, University of Texas at Austin) in Jakarta in December 2008. All stakeholders identified by CI were present except, critically, representatives of the communities affected by MEDCO's proposed development. Both CI and MEDCO argued that it was logistically impossible to include the local communities at that stage. This was a glaring omission but two steps were taken to mitigate the ethical problems it raised: (1) MEDCO had canvassed community opinion to some extent before the meeting and the issues that were flagged were explicitly discussed and (2) the planners made a commitment to consult with the communities in developing a plan.

The plan was almost entirely based on remotely sensed data supplemented by known locations of biota of importance, especially vegetation assemblages of cultural significance (*sago* patches). The identification of biodiversity constituents (see below in the text) was done with due attention to normative issues: all the culturally significant species assemblages were slated for protection. Habitat types, largely defined by vegetation structure and composition, were used as biodiversity surrogates, and targets of representation within the conservation area network were set using a linear scale that gave higher priority to rarer types. The rarest habitat type had a target of 100 percent representation whereas the most common ones had targets of 10 percent.

Residents' preferences were finally given central importance while performing a multi-criteria analysis that was used to prioritize areas for conservation. (The prioritization was performed using the ConsNet software package.) As noted earlier, all *sago* patches were designated for conservation. Moreover, all villages were given a large buffer around them for potential future development (even though this was regarded as unlikely given demographic shifts away from rural areas in the region to urban and urbanizing areas); these buffer areas were excluded from plantation development but also not targeted for conservation. The arrangement of both conservation and plantation areas was made as spatially coherent as permissible under the constraints by giving high priority to connectivity and compactness, leading to larger contiguous areas. Finally, villages expressed a strong desire for having the conservation areas close to them for ease of access for non-timber products and other sustainable uses. This was given high priority.

A variety of plans (potential conservation area networks) ranked high by these criteria were created and presented to MEDCO for further consideration and refinement. While MEDCO promised implementation, the extent to which this will happen remains unknown.

is defined, and much of this chapter is concerned with that problem.

(2) It must be ensured that the biodiversity in the conservation area networks persists into the future. This is the goal of *persistence*. This is where conservation biology draws most significantly from traditional ecology, which provides models for temporal changes in species' populations and in the composition of ecological communities (consisting of interacting species). However, persistence depends as much on changes wrought by human modification of habitats either through direct intervention such as Land Use and Land Cover (LULC) change or through global transformations such as climate change. It is thus an interesting question whether conservation should primarily be viewed as a biological rather than a social science; as we shall see, there is an equally serious question about whether, because of issues connected with the definition of biodiversity, conservation must embrace norms and thus include humanistic concerns from philosophy, anthropology, *etc.*, beyond both the natural and social sciences.

(3) Conservation area networks should be designed with as much *economy* as possible. (Sometimes, this is referred to as "efficiency.") This goal is motivated by the realization that conservation for biodiversity is but one of many competing normatively legitimate claims on the use of land and oceans including (human) habitation, economic development (resource extraction, industrial transformation, *etc.*), or even the pursuit of other natural values (recall Chapter 2). Thus, setting aside conservation areas, and other actions, in the pursuit of conservation costs resources. Consequently, economy is at a premium in conservation planning. This means that, in general,

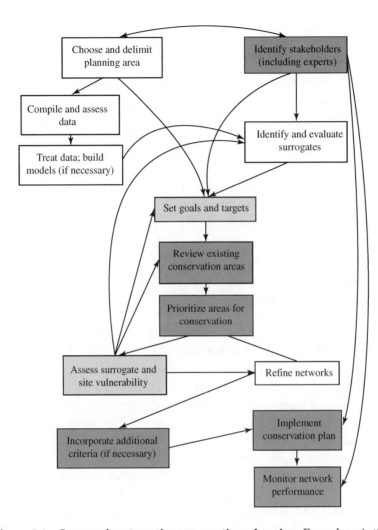

Figure 5.1   Stages of systematic conservation planning. For a description of the stages, see Table 5.1. Arrows indicate which components directly influence which others. Bidirectional arrows indicate feedback. Only the major interactions between the components are shown. There is potential for feedback between almost any two components of this framework. Boxes shaded in dark gray indicate aspects that are well understood; those with no shading are aspects that are fairly well understood; and those shaded in light gray are areas that remain poorly understood and subject to much ongoing research.

conservation area networks should occupy as little area as possible while satisfying the two other goals discussed earlier.

Arguably, systematic conservation planning is the most philosophically interesting part of conservation biology because of its scope: it raises all the philosophical issues that emerge from the larger discipline. Discussion of the representation goal raises all pertinent questions about biodiversity: what it means, how it should be defined, and how it should be measured. Because the analysis of persistence requires the use of ecological models, discussion of that goal potentially raises all issues in the philosophy of ecology, including the nature of ecological models, definitions of community, reductionism, *etc.* Notwithstanding their philosophical interest, these issues are beyond the explicit scope of this volume and will not be pursued here.[10] However, there are other interesting questions about persistence that are germane to the concerns of this book, especially how persistence should be defined, and these will merit discussion below. Finally, the goal of economy directly raises questions about making decisions that were discussed in Chapter 4, and indirectly reminds us that there remain fundamental unresolved disputes about the basis for conservation, issues that were discussed in Chapter 3.

The last point deserves emphasis. As Table 5.1 indicates, systematic conservation planning involves the explicit use of a decision-theoretic protocol (recall the discussion of Chapter 4). It requires the identification of agents (the stakeholders), explicit formulation of goals and representation targets, the formulation of potential plans (the alternatives), and multi-criteria analysis for the quantitative evaluation of the performance of these alternatives with respect to the goals, ideally incorporating all relevant uncertainties. Box 5.1 describes a typical systematic conservation planning exercise, recently carried out in the Merauke region of the Indonesian province of Papua (in New Guinea).

Ecological Diversity and Stability

Though conservation biology has emerged as a discipline that is distinct from ecology, the latter discipline should not be ignored completely in philosophical discussions of biodiversity conservation. The reason for this is that ecologists have been dealing with the problem of defining *diversity* within their discipline for several decades.[11] Even though conservation biologists paid little attention to these discussions when the term "biodiversity" was being introduced and popularized, this earlier (and often quite conceptually sophisticated) work provides a standard to which the concept of *biodiversity* can be usefully compared.

Within ecology, diversity was regarded as important because a highly influential speculation of twentieth-century ecologists has been the claim that diversity begets stability in ecological communities. This claim was made precise by Robert MacArthur's brilliant mathematical work in the 1950s.[12] Some initial empirical support for this claim was provided by the work of Charles Elton and David Pimentel in the early 1960s but, over the next decade, this support became questionable and eventually largely evaporated.[13] To make matters worse, in the 1970s, Robert May constructed mathematical models that purported to show that more complex (which may be interpreted as more diverse) communities were less stable than simpler ones.[14] There have been many responses to May's work, none definitive. The debate remains unresolved today.

In fact, the debate may prove to be impossible to resolve, either theoretically or empirically (in the field). The reason is that there are so many different concepts of diversity and stability that the number of possible combinations to be tested soon becomes astronomical. Let us begin with diversity. One obvious concept is *richness*: the number of species in a community. However, this does not exhaust what we may mean by diversity. Consider two communities, A and B. Let each have 100 individuals belonging to two species, κ and λ. In A, 50 individuals belong to species κ and 50 belong to λ. However, in B, 99 belong to κ and only one belongs to λ. Both A and B have a richness of 2, yet there is an obvious sense in which A is more diverse than B. What we are invoking here is a second concept of diversity: *evenness* or *equitability*. Now, almost all discussions of the diversity–stability relationship have interpreted diversity as richness. But there is no conceptual reason for this restriction and, given the stalemate in the debate, no empirical reason either.

Besides richness and equitability, there are at least four other concepts of diversity:[15]

- *Average abundance rarity*, with more diverse communities being those that have more species with low relative abundance.
- *Geographical rarity*, with more diverse communities being those that have more geographically rare species.
- *Distinctiveness*, with more diverse communities being those that are richer in phenotypically or taxonomically peculiar species.
- *Abundance transfer*, in which diversity increases when the population size of a more common species decreases alongside an increase in the population size of a rarer species.

These six concepts have been operationalized by at least 16 different definitions that can be used to estimate them in the field; many of these definitions attempt to incorporate more than one concept.

Turning to stability, by some classifications there may be as many as 70 concepts sharing 163 definitions between them.[16] The number of concepts may, with some effort, be reduced to seven:

- *Local stability*: The probability of a system's return to a reference state after a small perturbation.
- *Resilience*: Defined alternatively as the rate of a return to a reference state after a perturbation or as the probability of an eventual return after a perturbation.
- *Resistance*: The size of the change in an ecological community's properties from which it can recover.
- *Perturbation tolerance*: The size of the overall perturbation from which a community can recover.
- *Persistence*: The ability of a community to continue doing what it is doing.

- *Constancy*: The absence of change.
- *Reliability*: The probability that a community will continue "functioning."

We now have anything between 42 (6 × 7) and 2608 (16 × 163) potential diversity–stability relationships to be investigated. Little wonder, then, that there is no end in sight for the diversity–stability debate. Had the diversity–stability relationship been canonized it would have been of immense importance for biodiversity conservation. Suppose that it is empirically established that high diversity leads to high stability; that is, the continued existence of ecological communities and the species occurring in them. Assuming that such stability is desirable, the supposed relation between diversity and stability would effectively underpin the rationale for conserving biodiversity (interpreted as the relevant diversity concept) beyond the discussions of Chapter 3. Unfortunately, that option is not available to environmentalists.

Complementarity[17]

In spite of these extended discussions, with the exception of richness, biodiversity, as conceptualized within the discipline of conservation biology, has made little use of these concepts of ecological diversity.[18] This may have been because conservation biologists thought they were doing something fundamentally new, unrelated to traditional academic ecology. Alternatively, it may have been because the stalemate in the diversity–stability debate had led to the community implicitly concluding that there was little value in these concepts of diversity. Or, perhaps, it could have been because all concepts of diversity other than richness are in practice much more difficult to operationalize for measurement in the field. As noted earlier (in Chapter 4), environmental problems, including those about biodiversity conservation, often require rapid decisions even in the presence of uncertainty. Consequently, adequate definitions of biodiversity must be easily operationalizable for use in the field. (All of these factors likely played a role.[19])

Species richness, however, was routinely used as a measure of the biodiversity of a region, presumably because of its simplicity (in terms of understanding both what it means and how it should be measured). It continues to be widely used today but there is a serious problem associated with it. Consider three units, A, B, and C. (These may be habitat parcels, communities, *etc.*) Suppose that A has a richness of 79 (that is, it has 79 species). Suppose that B has a richness of 58, and C one of 20. Now, if we measure diversity by richness, then A and B have the highest diversity and, if we were only able to protect two of the units (because of budget constraints, *etc.*), we would select them. But it turns out that A and B share 50 species in common, whereas both A and C as well as B and C only share one species in common. Clearly, given that A has been slated for conservation, there is a sense in which C contributes higher diversity than B. Similarly, given B, C contributes higher diversity than A. Finally, given C, A contributes higher diversity than B. Here, diversity is being interpreted as *complementarity* in its simplest form: what *new* elements a unit contributes to a reference set of units. When no reference set of units already exists (or, equivalently, it is the null set), complementarity reduces to richness. But, after the first unit is introduced into the reference set, complementarity is in general different from richness.

The concept of complementarity was introduced independently at least four times in the 1980s, in Australia, South Africa, and the United Kingdom. It turns out that, though conservation biologists were apparently unaware of this, it had its antecedents in a different discussion of ecological diversity than the one that led to the diversity–stability debate (see the last section). In the 1960s Whittaker distinguished between α-diversity, or diversity within a study area; β-diversity, or diversity between study areas; and γ-diversity, or the total diversity of a region (encompassing all the study areas).[20] Now, all the definitions of diversity considered in the last section (and relevant to the diversity–stability debate) only address α-diversity. In contrast, complementarity is conceptually related to β-diversity:[21] given some unit, A, if we are comparing two units, B and C, complementarity measures the extent of the difference between B or C on the one hand and A on the other. However, because the complementarity value of a unit is defined relative to a reference set, it is not identical to β-diversity. Compared to α-diversity, within ecology, there have been few quantitative definitions proposed for β-diversity or γ-diversity; however, those that have been proposed for β-diversity do not involve such a relativization. Thus, complementarity is related to, but not identical to, β-diversity.

In the design of conservation area networks, complementarity is a subsidiary goal that simultaneously serves the general goals of representation and economy: if there is high complementarity between the units of a network, any targeted representation of biodiversity is typically achieved with high economy because units are as different from each other as possible. Complementarity has been used to specify algorithms for the selection of conservation area networks. (The development of such algorithms has been a central research problem within systematic conservation planning, underscoring the point that conservation biology is a hybrid discipline incorporating insights from many fields; in this case, computer science and operations research.[22]) The basic idea is straightforward: pick the first unit of the network on the basis of richness (as noted earlier, complementarity reduces to richness in this case). Then iteratively pick units to maximize complementarity at each stage. It turns out that this algorithm comes very close to achieving optimal economy, but it is not perfect (see the "Economy" section later in this chapter).

Constituents and Surrogates[23]

Let us return to the fundamental question: what is biodiversity? Even a cursory survey of professional papers or textbooks of conservation biology will reveal two canonical definitions; they will also reveal almost no research that uses these definitions. The canonical definitions are the following:

(1) Biodiversity refers to the variety of life at every level of structural, taxonomic, and functional organization.
(2) Biodiversity refers to diversity of genes (alleles), species, and ecosystems.

Many conservation biologists, especially in moments of unbridled political advocacy, may endorse definition (1) but, if the term "biodiversity" is to reflect the practice of conservation biology, this definition is useless. Biodiversity, as Takacs has pointed out, becomes all of biology.[24] It is absurd to think that we should—let alone that we can—protect all diversity of structure, taxonomy, and function. We would have to protect almost every biotic entity. Biodiversity conservation is not the only policy goal in any social context, and resources for it are obviously not unlimited. Consequently, biotic features must be prioritized and an adequate definition of "biodiversity" must reflect where a society's priorities lie with respect to the type of biological diversity that deserves the most attention. We cannot reasonably aim to protect every biotic entity, even in principle.

Definition (2) was probably never intended to define "biodiversity" fully; rather, it was supposed to operationalize it in the sense that protecting these three categories would presumably protect most of what is intended to be captured by definition (1). The trouble is that it has been a rather unsuccessful operationalization: allelic diversity is almost impossible to estimate accurately or protect in natural populations; species diversity, if we really mean *all* species, including microbial species, is almost as intractable.

In practice, conservation biologists work with either limited sets of taxa or ecosystem types (for instance, vegetation types). However, it is often unclear whether the choice of limited sets of taxa or ecosystem types is motivated by practical considerations of measuring biodiversity or whether it reflects what biodiversity is categorically supposed to be. It is important to introduce a critical distinction at this state:

(a) *Biodiversity constituents* are those features of biota that are taken to define what biodiversity is. Definition (1) is one possibility but, for the problems noted above, it is not a particularly cogent definition. The next section turns to some common definitions.

(b) *Biodiversity surrogates* are features that can be measured (estimated and quantified) in the field that may be used in place of the constituents during conservation planning.

Once biodiversity constituents are selected, the question of whether a biodiversity surrogate set is adequate is a technical problem that is solved through what is called surrogacy analysis. There are many methods of surrogacy analysis but they all reflect one central idea: a surrogate set is adequate only if a conservation plan using the surrogates is very close (preferably identical) to the plan that would have resulted through the use of the constituents themselves. One important result has been that environmental parameters (soil type, climatic variables, topographic variables) are good surrogates for many taxa (the constituents).

What Is Biodiversity?

But what are these constituents, the "real" components of biodiversity? Definition (1) of the last section has obvious virtues but, as we saw, remains unworkable in practice. But, once we must select among biotic entities, there is no obvious answer and, more importantly, no technical answer to the question. Rather, any answer will involve a social choice based on cultural values. This does not mean that the choice is arbitrary; rather, the choice must be made on the basis of normative discussions that may well reflect our deepest values about what we want to do with the habitats for which we are responsible. Moreover, recalling that the concept of biodiversity was introduced in the context of an emerging science of conservation biology dedicated to its protection, and recognizing that the new concept must be understood in that context, there are four constraints on what any definition of "constituent" should satisfy:

(1) *The constituent set must consist of biotic features*: Since we are dealing with *bio*diversity it seems reasonable to restrict potential constituents to biotic features. This excludes, for instance, viewing environmental parameters as biodiversity constituents even though they may be adequate surrogates.

(2) *The variability of features must be captured*: This constraint reflects the fact that we are dealing with bio*diversity*. The emphasis should be on the differences between taxa or communities partly captured, for instance, by the concept of complementarity, which can potentially be used to quantify several potential biodiversity constituent sets.

(3) *Taxonomic spread is important*: Once again, since biodiversity constituents are supposed to capture diversity, they must be inclusive of a variety of taxa.[25]

(4) *Concern should not be limited to material resource use*: This is perhaps the least obvious of the constraints and its satisfaction may not be entirely indispensable. However, conservation biology emerged in a context in which there was overwhelming concern about the disappearance of species that had no ordinary "resource value"; that is, were not required for the satisfaction of tangible needs. In this context, a concept of biodiversity constituents that included "non-resource" biota would be preferable to one that did not.

Such constraints are called "adequacy conditions" by philosophers. They are supposed to be minimal constraints: a proposed definition that does not satisfy the constraints is deemed not adequate though the satisfaction of the constraints does not by itself guarantee that the definition is adequate. All four conditions are consistent with the tempered anthropocentrism position discussed in Chapter 3; however, intrinsic-value advocates have tended to emphasize the fourth condition more than their anthropocentric counterparts.

At least in practice, perhaps the most popular definition of biodiversity constituents characterizes them as all at-risk species (or other taxa). For instance, in the United States, the Endangered Species Act (ESA) targets endangered and threatened species for protection though attention is restricted to vertebrate and plant species. The most influential transnational conservation NGO, Conservation International, targets the World Conservation Union (IUCN) Red List species and endemic species. At the international transgovernmental level the IUCN Red List is perhaps the most important arbiter of what nations find important to conserve. This definition trivially satisfies the first three adequacy criteria. Since being at risk of extinction is not conceptually related to whether a biotic entity is perceived as a material resource, the fourth condition is also satisfied. What cultural values does this definition reflect? This question reflects more attention that it has received. One possibility is that species are being regarded as analogous to individuals who deserve protection in liberal democracy. Another possibility is that, in the 1960s (the period that led to the ESA in the United States), preventing extinction was seen as a component of a general cultural choice to prevent irreversible environmental loss through the consumption of non-renewable resources, air and water pollution, *etc*. Yet another possibility is that the focus on species simply goes back to the Biblical tradition of the Hebrew god's injunction to Noah.

An obvious alternative definition of biodiversity constituents characterizes them as all (ecological) community types (sometimes called habitat types). This is the strategy followed by The Nature Conservancy, an influential NGO, in the United States and several other countries. Table 5.2 lists various possibilities and their rationales. Perhaps the most interesting of these are sacred groves, which, for instance in the Indian state of Meghalaya (see Box 5.2), have emerged as candidates for conservation. Assuming that the groves refer to living forests or trees, they satisfy the biota adequacy criterion. In

Box 5.2   The Sacred Groves of Meghalaya[26]

In many areas of the world, including many parts of Africa and Asia, cultural groups maintain sacred groves, which are patches of forest that are preserved for religious or other spiritual reasons. These exist in almost all sub-Saharan African countries, particularly Ghana and Kenya. They are widespread in South Asia, particularly in the Western Ghats mountain range along the west coast of India and in the northeastern hill state of Meghalaya. The management of sacred groves varies from region to region. In most African cases, a targeted tree species or a small set of such species is protected. In the Western Ghats and Meghalaya, the entire ecological community is protected and the sacred groves are typically the only intact forests left in the landscape. In the Western Ghats, the remnant tropical wet forests of the region, which were decimated for timber during British colonial times and later, are protected. In Meghalaya, the unique cloud forests of the region are protected; together, the 79 sacred groves comprise over 25 000 ha. These are evergreen forests on a landscape dominated by limestone. Much of the ecology of the region continues to be devastated through coal mining and quarrying for limestone besides swidden farming with an increasingly shorter cycle (five years in 2000 compared to 30 years in 1900). Traditionally each village had at least one sacred grove but local traditions were largely destroyed by the activity of Christian missionaries from the 1840s onwards. Not one of the sacred groves has been systematically inventoried, other than for major tree species, but they are known to be particularly rich in amphibian species with a high degree of microendemism. At least 18 IUCN Red List amphibian species occur in this region. Cave invertebrates in the many caves and fissures under the ground have not been inventoried at all.

Some of the best-known sacred groves of Meghalaya are in the Khasi Hills near the town of Sohra (formerly known as Cherrapunji), which, with an average annual rainfall of 11 430 mm, is one of the wettest places on Earth. (The wettest is nearby Mawsynram.) Most groves are small and occur on the top of hills but the larger ones also include valleys and the streams that run through them. The most impressive grove here is at Mawphlong, which is protected because it is supposed to be inhabited by the spirit U Basa. Its 80 ha contain at least 400 tree species; the fauna have never been inventoried. The protection regime (known as "Kw'Law Lyngdoh") is severe: not even deadwood may be removed. The land around the grove is severely degraded. There is a minor ongoing restoration project sponsored by Community Forest International (and partly funded by USAID). It aims to pay 20 US dollars per hectare for the restoration of core forests, 10 US dollars per hectare for forest extension, and 2.5 US dollars per hectare for watershed management. It is also working towards the closure of mines and quarries in the surrounding area and has begun to focus on alternative job creation.

those cases the groves are entire communities and not just groupings of single targeted species; they also satisfy the variety adequacy criteria. If all the biota are targeted for protection, rather than individual sacred species, the "all taxa" criterion similarly is satisfied. The "sacred" probably never refers to ordinary material needs.[27]

Persistence

The whole point of biodiversity conservation is to ensure the persistence of biodiversity. We noted earlier that there is room for argument as to whether the problem of devising strategies to

Table 5.2 Biodiversity Constituent Sets

Constituent Set	Goal	Biota	Variability	Taxa	Beyond Material Resource	Cultural Values
At-risk taxa	Species and other taxa that have a high probability of extinction	√	√	√	√	Protection of individuals / Prevention of natural degradation / Noah principle
Community types	All habitat types at appropriate classification	√	√	√	√	All landscapes/seascapes have value
Charismatic taxa	Taxa that are of cultural significance	√	√	?*	√	Any value that determines cultural significance
Sacred groves	Habitat patch deemed sacred	√	√	√	√	Religious values defining sacredness

√ Indicates that the relevant adequacy criterion is satisfied by this constituent set.

* It is unlikely that most invertebrate taxa would ever be considered charismatic. (Butterflies are an obvious exception.)

achieve persistence is primarily a socio-political problem or a biological problem. Even if we decide in favor of biology, social values once again become critical in measuring success; in conservation biology philosophy apparently cannot be avoided. Values enter in answering two questions that cannot be avoided:

- *What level of risk is acceptable?* A typical answer has been that anything higher than a 5 percent probability of extinction within 1000 years is unacceptable. But neither of the figures—5 percent nor 1000 years—have any justification beyond the fact that their proponents find them reasonable. In other words, this is a social choice and any potential justification must be normative and should be based on an explicit discussion of social values.
- *What should the planning horizon be?* Given the amount of uncertainty that there is with respect to our environmental future, including what will become technologically feasible, is a horizon of 1000 years really appropriate? Or, is any prediction about the fate of a species (or other feature) that far into the future essentially nonsense? It is equally plausible to argue that all we should be concerned about is the state in which we leave our environment to the next generation. There are three considerations that support this position: (1) we may be able to predict the results of our policies with reasonable confidence; (2) policies should be revised iteratively as often as feasible because of unpredicted environmental, socio-political, and technological changes; and (3) we do not know what future generations will value and should not presume that our valuations reflect their preferences. Once again, we are back to discussing normative questions that properly belong in philosophy rather than the biological or social sciences.

Values aside, the biological difficulties of answering questions of persistence should also not go entirely unmentioned. Since the late 1970s biologists have been attempting to predict the probability of survival, expected time to extinction, and other similar parameters for at-risk species' populations so that these results can be used to inform conservation planning. These techniques are generally known as population viability analysis (PVA) and a large variety of software packages are available as decision support tools.[28] The trouble is that reliable viability analyses are "data hungry"; that is, they require a large amount of demographic and other data, which are available for only a handful of well-studied species in the North. For instance, with the exception of Australia, in tropical countries, which have the highest levels of species richness, such data are almost never available. Consequently, predicting persistence from biological models is well-nigh impossible in practice.

This is one reason why many conservation scientists have lately been suggesting that the problem be approached from a different perspective: that of modeling the threat (from, for instance, potential industrial or agricultural development) to habitats and using those results to make some assessment of the prognosis for biota. The trouble is that modeling threat accurately may turn out to be no easier than performing PVAs.

Reserves versus Conservation Areas[29]

What we have been calling conservation areas throughout this chapter were traditionally called reserves (for instance, in the early literature on conservation biology). It is worth briefly noting why the older terminology is being rejected and is gradually disappearing from the field. A conservation area is defined as any area that is managed with the persistence of biodiversity as one of its explicit goals. Achieving the goal of persistence may require management as a reserve but it may also be possible to achieve this goal under a variety of other management regimes including, for instance, traditional sericulture or pisciculture. (Sometimes, persistence may even require intrusive management for human use—recall Box 2.1's discussion of Keoladeo Ghana National Park in India.) The point is that this is an empirical question that must be determined through ecological studies. The conservation biology of the past often assumed *a priori* that the persistence of biodiversity required the creation of reserves without human presence, and these were sometimes implemented through the expulsion of people. Not only were such moves empirically unsupported, but the ethical problems should be obvious. The decision to identify conservation areas, rather than reserves, is largely motivated by the goal of moving beyond this legacy.

Economy

Recall that the three goals of systematic conservation planning were the maximization of representation, persistence, and economy. This means that planning can be conceptualized as solving a complex mathematical optimization problem during the design of conservation area networks: representation and persistence, as quantified through some suitable measures, would be maximized while maximal economy would simultaneously be achieved through minimization of some cost function. With respect to representation and economy, the planning process is increasingly being approached in this way in most regions of the world and, in the process, an elaborate conceptual framework accompanied by sophisticated computer algorithms has been developed for decision support. Persistence has largely been only informally incorporated, not because it is not recognized as being critically important but because persistence measures have been difficult to devise and compute when we have to cope with large numbers of biodiversity constituents (as noted in the last section).

Restricting attention to representation and economy, assume that for each surrogate to be represented in a conservation area network we have an explicit target of representation. This target could be the number of different populations of a species, the fraction of the habitat of some species, or the fraction of the total area occupied by some community, *etc.* Clearly, the goal of achieving persistence should guide what these targets should be but, for the reasons discussed earlier (in the "Persistence" section), planners have had to rely on heuristic ecological rules rather than ecological models to specify these targets. The optimization problem has been interpreted in two ways, each of which has many variants:[30]

- *The minimum area problem*: Select habitat parcels in such a way as to minimize their total area while satisfying the representation target for each surrogate.
- *The maximum representation problem*: Given a budgeted area (which can be put under a conservation plan), select habitat areas in such a way as to maximize the number of surrogates that meet their representation targets.

Both of these are mathematical problems that have been extensively studied within operations research.

In practice, the maximum representation problem is the one most often encountered because budget constraints are an ubiquitous part of the world. Strangely, the minimum area problem has been more extensively studied (Figure 5.2 shows an example). Solving these problems requires devising algorithms. Thus, in conservation biology, like computer science and unlike most of ecology, theoretical research consists of devising algorithms rather than formulating models and theories. In fact, because a variety of algorithms can be used to solve these problems, a lot of theoretical debate in conservation biology has been about the choice of algorithms.[31] For instance, one school has advocated the use of exact algorithms that guarantee that the optimal solution will be found but that often take a lot of computation time and are otherwise difficult to use. An opposing school has argued that fast heuristic algorithms that typically generate near-optimal solutions are more appropriate, particularly since what is likely to be implemented through a political decision process will never be the exact results of any algorithm. The most useful such heuristic is complementarity: if complementarity is maximized at each stage when selecting habitat patches for conservation, near-optimal solutions are usually found. Yet another school has recently proposed the use of a new class of "metaheuristic" algorithms that apply a heuristic rule repeatedly in order to improve performance. These algorithms are faster than exact algorithms while almost always producing optimal or near-optimal solutions. No immediate resolution seems forthcoming in this partly epistemological debate.

124

Figure 5.2 Representation of endemic mammals of México in a nominal conservation area network.[8] Solution of the minimum area problem for México. The country was divided into 71 248 cells, each 0.05° × 0.05° (of longitude and latitude), for this exercise; then, 86 endemic species were used as biodiversity constituents because no conservation plan for México can reasonably ignore species that are endemic to that country. The target was set as 10 percent of the habitat of each such species and an optimal solution was then found (consisting of the black cells in the figure). It turns out that there are a large number of optimal plans (each selecting the same total area), which vary considerably on how the selected cells are spatially distributed. The solution was found using the ConsNet software package, which implements a metaheuristic algorithm called "tabu search."

The Significance of Algorithms and Software Decision Support Tools

As noted earlier, systematic conservation planning advocates—and often presumes—the use of software decision support tools often incorporating sophisticated algorithms for area selection, sometimes including explicit multi-criteria analysis. A wide variety of such tools have been created during the last two decades and their popularity is increasing.[32] The use of these tools replaces the earlier strategy of

125

relying on the educated intuition of experts (though some organizations such as The Nature Conservancy have continued the earlier practice of using expert opinion).

Two aspects of the emergence of algorithmic methods are philosophically worth noting. First, one explicit goal of developing these methods was to make planning exercises repeatable. Different sets of individuals analyzing the same information should produce identical plans. As noted in Chapter 4, this is a central virtue of formal decision theory. This goal is the analog of the standard requirement in the empirical sciences that an experiment be repeatable by different experimenters and must yield the same result for it to be trusted.

Second, and equally important, as philosophers should continually be reminded, intuitions can be mistaken. An example will illustrate this point. In 2000, a conservation plan was developed for several hundred at-risk species in Québec by solving various versions of the minimum area problem.[33] While a variety of targets of representation were explored for these species, all analyses routinely selected several small islands in the Gulf of St. Lawrence as part of a conservation area network. Yet, a group of experts who had considered the problem earlier had never targeted these islands. It turned out that the islands provided habitat for nesting pairs of several endangered bird species. In retrospect, the experts fully concurred with the results produced by the algorithms. But, in their earlier considerations, their expert intuitions had simply ignored islands. Intuitions are fallible in a way algorithms are not. This observation is not intended to suggest that algorithms should be used blindly. They can fall afoul of every error in the data, however obvious those may be to an expert. Algorithms are useful for decision *support*, not decision making.

Beyond the use of algorithms, does the fact that they are implemented in software make any real difference? Conceptually, it does not.[34] Dedicated software packages allow large data sets to be analyzed efficiently, many of which, involving thousands of species, landscapes, and seascapes divided into millions of cells, could never be reasonably analyzed by hand. That is the value of these dedicated software packages. But these software packages also come accompanied by a new worry. The results are often visually persuasive maps that prompt acceptance—and reification—of results without due scrutiny. Typically these software packages are embedded in geographic information systems, which make non-trivial ontological assumptions about the organization of the world.[35] The conclusion to draw is that algorithm and software results should be treated with cautious respect and experts should try to understand why the results are what they are.

Notes

1. For histories of different aspects of conservation biology, from different disciplinary perspectives, see Soulé (1987) (a conservation biology perspective), Takacs (1996) (science studies), Sarkar 1998b, 2005) (philosophy), and Kingsland (2002) (history).
2. Sarkar (2007b) elaborates on this development.
3. For more on this point, see Sarkar (2002).
4. The medical analogy is deep and goes back to Soulé (1985); see also Sarkar (2002).
5. This development can be dated back to an important early manifesto—see Lubchenco *et al.* (1991).
6. This example is from recently concluded field work (Sarkar, unpublished data; see also Conservation Internation, 2010).
7. The treatment follows Sarkar and Illoldi-Rangel (2010) in most details. That work is a modification of Margules and Sarkar (2007).
8. Figure redrawn using data from Ciarleglio *et al.* (2009).
9. For details on systematic conservation planning beyond the discussion here and in Table 5.1, see Margules and Pressey (2000), who introduce the goals of representation and persistence, and Margules and Sarkar (2007), who also include economy.
10. Odenbaugh (2005) provides a useful entry into that literature.
11. The argument of this section is elaborated in Sarkar (2007b).
12. See, especially, MacArthur (1955).
13. See Elton (1958) and Pimentel (1961); Pimm (1991) summarizes the empirical work of the next decade.

14. See May (1973). A detailed analysis of the response to May's work is yet to be written.
15. The analysis follows Patil and Taillie (1982) and Sarkar (2010a). For a more empirically oriented review, see Magurran (1988) for the early period and Magurran (2003) for an update.
16. Grimm and Wissel (1997) provide a catalog.
17. The term was first introduced by Vane-Wright *et al.* (1991). For a detailed historical analysis, on which this section is based, see Justus and Sarkar (2002).
18. For an emphasis on diversity as richness, in spite of the problems noted here, see MacLaurin and Sterelny (2008).
19. On this point, see the discussion of Sarkar (2007b).
20. Whittaker (1960); for details of this history, see Sarkar (2007b).
21. Magurran (2003) was the first to note this relationship explicitly; however, she does not note the way in which the two concepts (complementarity and β-diversity) do differ, as explained in the text.
22. The philosophical significance of the use of these algorithms is discussed in the last section of this chapter.
23. The analysis presented in the rest of this chapter was gradually developed by Sarkar (2002), Sarkar and Margules (2002), and Sarkar (2008).
24. See Takacs (1996).
25. Depending on how criterion (2) is interpreted, criterion (3) may already be implied by it. However, it may be the case that measures of variability do not adequately capture the unique significance of all taxa. For instance, a measure could result in a higher value for a system with every vertebrate species, but with no fungi, compared to one with a moderate number of both vertebrate species and fungi.
26. Details are from Malhotra *et al.* (2007) and fieldwork (Sarkar, unpublished data).
27. Woods (2000) takes yet another approach and construes biodiversity as an environmental condition.
28. See Gilpin and Soulé (1986) and Boyce (1992). Population viability analyses and their history are discussed in some detail by Sarkar (2005).
29. This argument was elaborated in Sarkar (2003). While "conservation area" was being used even earlier, the explicit rejection of "reserve" seems to have been first promoted in that piece.
30. The discussion follows Sarkar *et al.* (2004), as modified in Margules and Sarkar (2007).

31. For a review, see Sarkar *et al.* (2006).
32. These have been reviewed by Sarkar *et al.* (2006) and Moilanen *et al.* (2009).
33. This example is from Sarakinos *et al.* (2001).
34. Margules and Sarkar (2007) emphasize this point.
35. This problem has been discussed in some detail by Sarkar (2005, pp. 131–132).

6

Environmental Restoration

As human activity continues to degrade more and more land and seascapes, there remain progressively fewer relatively intact areas that can plausibly be managed for the conservation of existing natural values. Benign neglect is no longer an option, whether we are interested in preventing the extinction of species or ensuring that ecosystem services remain intact. Moreover, merely managing conserved lands will also not suffice to maintain an adequate complement of natural values in many contexts: not enough relatively intact habitats remain. Left with no other choice in their pursuit of natural values, in recent years environmentalists have broached the problems of reconstructing habitats to enhance natural values (including many of those that were discussed in Chapter 2). This is hardly a novel goal. It has probably been part of human culture ever since the invention of settled agriculture required the active management of land to ensure continued productivity. However, as in other environmental contexts, the nineteenth and twentieth centuries have seen the development of some distinctive practices to achieve this goal; the late twentieth century has also seen the formulation of an explicit conceptual framework and the creation of an academic discipline, *restoration ecology*, dedicated to this goal.[1]

The most interesting philosophical problems that arise in the context of habitat reconstruction are normative. When should we bother with habitat reconstruction? What should the goals of

Environmental Philosophy: From Theory to Practice, First Edition. Sahotra Sarkar.
© 2012 John Wiley & Sons Inc. Published 2012 by John Wiley & Sons Inc.

reconstruction be? How should we judge success? Should we ever intervene to alter natural habitats? Except for the last, none of these questions has so far received the philosophical attention each deserves, though the situation is changing. (Historians are also only beginning to focus on restoration ecology.) We begin this chapter by noting the context in which restoration ecology emerged in north America in the 1980s, though many early insights came from developments in Britain. In particular, we pay attention to the controversies over the definition of ecological restoration, the dominant mode of habitat reconstruction that environmentalists advocate today. We then explore the question of goals, first within the constraints of ecological restoration and then more generally when we embrace a wider set of natural values as goals for the reconstruction of habitats. Then we turn to the questions of judging success and justifying anthropogenic intervention to "improve" nature.

Before we begin, it is worth noting that the normative justification for reconstruction is usually presumed to be necessarily anthropocentric because humans choose which natural values to promote. However, this assumption is flawed. There may be contexts in which we could direct our reconstruction efforts towards what may loosely be called restitution: restoration of (non-human) entities to ensure the enhancement of their intrinsic value. Thus, even though reconstruction would be proximately guided by human values, the ultimate goal would not be determined by these values. We will not pursue this line of argument any further because, as we saw in Chapter 3, there is no compelling argument to attribute intrinsic value to entities such as habitats or ecological communities (which are the typical loci of interest for reconstruction).

Ecological Restoration[2]

In the north American context it is customary to trace back restoration efforts to the work of Aldo Leopold in the first half of the twentieth century, but the distinctive practices that came to be called ecological restoration only emerged in the 1970s, drawing primarily on work both in Britain and the United States.[3] Institutionally, the field came to be firmly established with the formation of the Society for Ecological Restoration (SER) in 1988 with its own journal, *Restoration Ecology*, which began publication in 1992. The term "restoration" replaced a wide variety of terms that had been used during the previous few decades to describe a set of similar practices: reclamation, reconstruction, regeneration, rehabilitation, revegetation, *etc.*

What "restoration" should mean was actively debated by its practitioners throughout the 1980s and 1990s. Should it embrace all the practices mentioned in the last paragraph? Or should it be something much more narrow? There was widespread disagreement. For instance, in 1992, a Committee on Restoration of Aquatic Ecosystems appointed by the US National Research Council canvassed the literature and came up with 60 different definitions.[4] The SER also produced three separate definitions, including two influential ones in 1996 and 2002, based on input from internal Science and Policy working groups.

The 1996 and 2002 SER definitions differ significantly. In 1996, the SER claimed: "Ecological restoration is the process of assisting the recovery and management of ecological integrity." The 2002 definition drops the reference to integrity: "Ecological restoration is the process of assisting the recovery of an ecosystem that has been degraded, damaged, or destroyed." For many SER members the reference to ecological integrity was an unwarranted abstraction to be avoided. For them, the 2002 definition brought the discipline back to what practitioners were doing in the field.[5]

Nevertheless, Eric Higgs, a philosopher and restoration ecologist who was one of those responsible for formulating these definitions, has urged that both recovery, presumably to a past state (what Higgs and a primer produced by the SER both call "historical fidelity"), and ecological integrity should be goals of restoration. This characterization is also more consistent than the 2002 SER definition with the definition produced by the US National Research Council *restoration* . . . is defined as the return of an ecosystem to a close approximation of its condition prior to disturbance. . . . Both the structure and the function of the ecosystem are recreated. . . . The goal is to emulate a natural, functioning, self-regulating system that is integrated with the ecological landscape in which it occurs.

In what follows we shall look at both historical fidelity and integrity.

Reference States and Dynamics

We will focus on Higgs' characterization of ecological restoration below.[6] It appears to capture two features that may be critical to any definition of habitat reconstruction. But note, first, that the term "habitat reconstruction" is being construed here as being more general than ecological restoration, including in its ambit all practices that self-consciously modify habitats to enhance natural values; restoration is just one form of reconstruction.

Returning to Higgs, and abstracting from his requirements of historical fidelity and ecological integrity, the two features that seem to characterize habitat reconstruction are: (1) a *reference state* must be specified as part of the goals of a reconstruction project and (2) a *reference dynamic* of process parameters must be similarly specified—the idea here is to ensure that the goals are not transient mirages but, rather, result in a system that continues to persist in the future. (Both are sometimes included in what are called *reference conditions* in work in restoration ecology.) If the reference state and dynamic are adequately reconstructed then, presumably, the system will evolve as desired, along what is sometimes called the *reference trajectory*.

Both the reference state and dynamic are criteria to be used to judge the performance of a reconstruction attempt. The reference state is defined by the composition of the system, the constituents of the ecological community, and the community's biophysical surroundings. The reference dynamic consists of the biophysical and ecological processes operating in the reconstructed system.

(Box 6.1 describes the choices in the ongoing reconstruction of the Florida Everglades in the United States, perhaps the most ambitious ecological restoration so far attempted—note how it is almost entirely concerned with the reference state except for maintaining a specified flow of water, which constitutes a reference dynamic for

Box 6.1   Restoration of the Florida Everglades[7]

Historically, the greater Everglades ecosystem consisted of 10 500 km^2 of southern Florida. It extended 200 km from north to south and measured about 80 km at its widest point. Its western boundary consisted of the Big Cypress Swamp; the eastern boundary consisted of the raised Atlantic Coastal Ridge. Lake Okeechobee, a wide and shallow lake (around 1900 km^2) averaging only 3.6 m in depth, formed the northern boundary; the southern boundary consisted of tidal mangrove forests on the tip of Florida. Lake Okeechobee in the north was a major source of water for the wetland, which, even today, consists of a patchwork of lakes and rivers, freshwater marshes, islands of trees, mangrove swamps, and coastal waters.

Today, less than half of the greater Everglades ecosystem remains, and even this remnant has to compete with urban and agricultural interests besides coping with polluted runoff from these activities. Alteration of this ecosystem began back in 1848 when reclamation proponents promised the US Congress that draining the wetland by between 1.5 and 2 m would produce a tropical breadbasket. However, reclamation proved difficult because of the terrain, including the dramatic seasonal and annual fluctuations of the water–land interface. Concerted drainage efforts only started in 1882. In 1907 a drainage district was created and, by the early 1930s, over 700 km of canals had been constructed, spurring human population growth along Florida's southeast coast.

Conservationists worried about what the destruction of the wetland would do to both fauna and flora and ecosystem functions. Their efforts to prevent complete destruction succeeded with the establishment of a park in 1934. However, the Everglades National Park was only dedicated in 1947 and comprised barely two-thirds of the original plan because of private land holdings.

Restoration efforts started as early as 1939 with a "re-watering" plan but only gained momentum after disastrous floods in 1947 and 1948. The US Army Corps of Engineers produced a Comprehensive Plan for the Everglades largely based on the 1939 re-watering plan; meanwhile, the US Congress established the Central and Southern Florida Project for Flood Control and Other Purposes. These initiatives were technology-driven, leading to the construction of levees, water channel "improvements," water storage, and the systematic use of massive water pumps to supplement drainage by gravity. A 160 km levee was constructed as a buffer between the Everglades and development while, at the same time, urban sprawl effectively destroyed $400 \, km^2$ of the remaining wetland. However, a significant part (roughly $4000 \, km^2$) of the Everglades was protected from further development. But the levees began to attract agricultural development in the northern Everglades above Lake Okeechobee, in the so-called Everglades Agricultural Area. Bitter disputes about water flow into the park erupted. These were resolved in the 1970s but the solution had little resemblance to the natural hydrological flow the region had once enjoyed. More engineered alterations of the natural hydrological flow occurred throughout the 1970s. Meanwhile, in 1974 the Big Cypress National Preserve was established. In 1976 UNESCO declared the Everglades National Park a Biosphere Reserve under its "Man and Biosphere" program. In 1979 UNESCO went further and declared the Everglades a World Heritage Site.

Major droughts and floods in 1980 and 1982 prompted the Everglades National Park to declare an environmental emergency and propose a plan to respond to its water-supply and water-control problems. In 1984 the US Congress passed an act that authorized these water deliveries and initiated an experiment to deliver the water in a fashion that mimicked rainfall patterns. Finally, multiple governmental agencies began to address the park's continued deterioration. In 1989 the US Congress authorized park expansion to the northeast though only in what was regarded as undevelopable land. A planning process was set into motion that eventually resulted in the 1999 Comprehensive Everglades Restoration Plan (CERP), specifying perhaps the most ambitious restoration project ever attempted anywhere. The general goal of the CERP was to restore, preserve, and protect the South Florida ecosystem while providing for other water-related needs of the region, including water supply and flood protection. Major components of CERP included:

- *Increase in water storage capacity*: A variety of water storage plans were envisioned, including storage of surface water and assisted aquifer recovery.
- *Improvements in water quality*: The main strategy would be the creation of water treatment wetlands along the periphery of the system. Water flow from urban areas to the Everglades would be controlled for quality.
- *Improved water deliveries to the estuaries and the Everglades*: This included improvements both in the quantity of water and the timing of deliveries, particularly to the Everglades National Park.
- *Restoration of the connectivity of the system*: Many of the levees and artificial canals would be removed and some natural ones recreated.

Independent of the CERP, additional restoration efforts for the Everglades included four other projects:

- *Modified Water Deliveries to Everglades National Park*: This, too, involved a return to traditional water flows in the region.
- *The C-111 Project*: This involved restoring the original hydrological conditions in several specified sectors in the region.
- *Kissimmee River Restoration Project*: The original conditions would be restored to an area that was once a large floodplain. The main strategies included removal of water control structures and restoration of part of the original canal network.
- *Everglades Construction Project*: The major strategy was the construction of new wetlands, designed in part to control the amount of phosphates entering the Everglades as a result of agricultural activities.

The bewildering variety of these projects underscores how complex restoration can be. Critics (such as Higgs) have found fault with the technological orientation of many of these efforts. But given the scale of the problem it is hard to see how massive technological intervention, if it is well-directed, can or should be avoided. The total cost is supposed to exceed eight billion dollars. Whether the initiatives will succeed remains to be seen.

this restoration effort.) The critical questions are whether historical fidelity is an appropriate guide for choosing a reference state, whether ecological integrity allows us to choose an appropriate reference dynamic, and, if not, whether there are other appropriate choices. However, before we turn to these questions in subsequent sections, two issues deserve mention.

First, it would be a mistake to view the reference state of a system as static. As noted in Chapter 2, ecological communities are dynamic entities, changing over time. This raises a problem, not easily resolved, as to how a reference state should be characterized. There are several options: the description may be general enough to permit considerable variability (*e.g.*, a specific fraction of forest cover or wetland, or specific values for hydrological parameters), the system may be underspecified (*e.g.*, only some species may be specified as having to occur), and so on. Yet another option is to suggest that a particular reference state be reached once but not that it be maintained: the reference dynamic then takes over. (The reference dynamic may also change over time.) There is as yet no consensus on these matters. What philosophical analysis does is to draw explicit attention to the problem.

Second, and this point has already been partly broached in the last paragraph, the reference state and reference dynamic cannot be completely decoupled from each other. The ecological constituents of the reference state will interact with each other and their biophysical surroundings. Conversely, to ensure that the appropriate processes occur in a system, it must have the appropriate constituents. One interesting question emerges: should reference states be selected first, thus constraining possible dynamics, or should it be the other way around? Once again, there is as yet no consensus about the answer.

Historical Fidelity

What distinguishes ecological restoration, as it is construed now, from other modes of habitat reconstruction is the use of historical fidelity to choose the reference state and ecological integrity to choose the reference dynamic. Now, what we aspire for in our habitats is determined by what we value: consequently, the issues that must be addressed here are unavoidably normative. In some contexts, circumstances pretty much dictate what we should value. If we are faced with food shortages, it would be strange—if not downright irrational—not to value productivity of our land. If we are facing problems with polluted water, it would similarly be strange not to reconstruct wetlands that would remove contaminants. In many other contexts, what should be valued is far less clear and must be decided through potentially contentious, but unavoidable, cultural discussion. Historical fidelity avoids much of this discussion by providing a veridical method to choose the reference state: that is what is supposed to be special about ecological restoration (compared to other types of habitat reconstruction).

Historical fidelity is not supposed to be interpreted as the exact replication of past systems, which would be practically impossible. Rather, it means approximate achievement of past conditions with contextual factors (such as the data available and the resources that can be dedicated to restoration) determining what degree of approximation is sufficient. The degree of approximation can be easily captured by explicitly indicating how much variability or underspecification is permissible in the reference state in the way indicated earlier.

Returning to the salient normative issue: why should we value historical fidelity? With the exception of Higgs' work mentioned earlier, there has been surprisingly little explicit philosophical (or other) discussion of this question. The term "restoration" itself may be at fault: the concept of restoration seems naturally to imply a past that has to be brought back, even though the practice of ecological restoration in the field often belies any such motivation, especially back when, in the pre-definitional era, restoration was seen to include reclamation, revegetation, and other similar practices. If the journal *Restoration Ecology* is any indication, practitioners of the discipline rarely pay much attention to the subtleties of achieving historical fidelity rather than some otherwise desirable natural state that, at most, pays lip service to historical antecedent. The example of the Florida Everglades (Box 6.1) illustrates the same point.[8] In other words, taking historical fidelity seriously and criticizing it as a goal may end up being a critique of the theory of ecological restoration but irrelevant to its practice. Nevertheless, for philosophical purposes, theory does matter, and we will proceed with a critical examination below. Perhaps the lesson to be learned—if the criticism can be sustained—is that the theory should be modified to be in better agreement with practice.

As noted earlier, Higgs has provided explicit philosophical arguments for historical fidelity. He offers three arguments: an endorsement of nostalgia, a claim that fidelity provides narrative continuity, and a claim that fidelity provides "depth of time," another claim that is supposed to be related to narrative continuity. But behind these explicit arguments runs a deeper worry: without historical fidelity restoration efforts may fall prey to caprice, whims of the moment determining what we should value and pursue in our restoration efforts. We will return to the important question of caprice later. First, let us examine the three explicit arguments:

(1) Neither Higgs nor any other advocate of historical fidelity endorses nostalgia without reservation, claiming that the past is always better than the present simply because it is the past.[9] Rather, the past is supposed to have *often* been better. A variety of reasons are supposed to show why this is so. For instance, Higgs argues that the past is often simpler than the present and, indeed, this is probably a common reason for nostalgia in many contexts, not just that of restoration. But it does not survive even mild scrutiny without a nuanced discussion of simplicity. A depauperate ecological community is simpler than one with more species, more complexity. Is this the type of simplicity we value? Perhaps sometimes, for instance, if what has come to "enrich" the system are species that are alien and are threatening the persistence of native species. But, then, what we really value are at-risk native species. This may be an argument for fidelity to native ecosystems, but it is not an argument for *historical* fidelity. Cultural simplicity does not fare any better: human well-being depends on the richness of daily interactions with others. Perhaps the most compelling argument for nostalgia is that ecosystems of the past had a higher degree of self-sustainability than systems that have been disrupted by human activity. This is plausible in many contexts and we will return to the desirability of self-sustainability later in this chapter—it fares better as a criterion for choosing the reference dynamic. Meanwhile, three reservations should be noted here: once again, what is at stake is not the value

of historical fidelity *per se* but rather self-sustainability. Whether the past state of a system was more self-sustainable than the present, or some other possible reconstructed future, is an empirical question. We cannot simply assume that the past system was better in this respect. Self-sustainability may not have characterized systems of the past, for instance, in the case of those systems that have co-evolved with human practices for millennia. In such cases self-sustainability may be completely irrelevant.

(2 and 3) We will deal with narrative continuity and depth of time together since they are closely related. Narrative continuity is supposed to mean that we know the history of a place, and there is more depth of time the longer the period for which that history is available. When places are embedded in such narratives, it is supposed to be easier to motivate people to carry out restoration. The last claim may well be true but, then, what matters is motivation, not historical fidelity *per se*. The argument also presumes that other sources of motivation are not equally effective; for instance, it would be harder to convince people to plant a communal garden that had nothing to do with the history of a place. There is an even deeper worry here. Being able to motivate people is clearly important in environmental contexts, both to enhance the feasibility of a plan and to get people used to working for the enhancement of natural values. Nevertheless, should what we set as our goals be so thoroughly dependent on this criterion? Or should we regard the desirability of motivating people as one of the many conditions that determine what course of action is feasible, which, in turn, may limit our expectations about the achievement of goals? The contrast here is with whether this criterion should influence what our goals should be in the first place.

The possibility of caprice provides a much more compelling rationale for historical fidelity. Preferences change over time; consequently, so do the goals of individuals (and groups). If historical fidelity ensures the selection of a particular historical ecosystem as the reference state, it does not change with possibly capricious variation in preferences. This seems plausible enough, but there are two sources of problems. The first is with respect to the choice of the historical ecosystem to be emulated. Ultimately this is a cultural

141

choice, not one dictated by any ecological fact. The second is that we must choose which aspects of a historical ecosystem to emulate. Ideally, we should emulate the entire ecosystem, but that is impossible in almost any context. Presumably we should choose *representative* aspects, but what is deemed representative is also a matter of choice. Both choices leave ample room for caprice.

Box 6.2 describes perhaps the most ambitious restoration plan ever proposed: the Pleistocene re-wilding of north America, which would involve the introduction of a huge number of non-native (African

Box 6.2 The Pleistocene Re-wilding of North America

In August 2005 a group of scientists—and one right-wing activist (Dave Foreman, erstwhile of Earth First!)—announced an ambitious restoration plan for north America.[10] They proposed to introduce and promote species supposedly closely related to north American megafauna from the late Pleistocene era, 13 000 million years ago. Partly, the goal was to prevent the global extinction of at-risk African and Asian species, including the Asian ass (*Equus hemionus*), Przewalski's horse (*Equus przewalskii*), Bactrian camel (*Camelus bactrianus*), African cheetah (*Acinonyx jubatus*), African elephant (*Loxodonta africana*), Asian elephant (*Elephas maximus*), and lion (*Panthera leo*). But the more important purpose was supposedly to restore the "evolutionary potential" of North American biota, and to assuage the guilt that the authors felt for the allegedly anthropogenic extinction of North American megafauna: "humans were probably at least partly responsible for the Late Pleistocene extinctions in North America, and our subsequent activities have curtailed the evolutionary potential of most remaining large vertebrates. We therefore bear an ethical responsibility to redress these problems."[11]

Within the conservation biology community the proposal was largely greeted with derision. There was also concern that conservation resources would be turned away from countries of the South in which the megafauna were under severe threat. The ethics of reallocating such resources away from the South, particularly from sub-Saharan Africa, had escaped the plan's proponents while they explored their moral responsibilities to long-extinct species. Biological critics pointed out that we do not know what such massive introductions of exotic species would do to habitats. Nor do we know enough about the Pleistocene era to judge whether we can recover its "evolutionary potential," even if we knew what this term means (which is less than clear). Critics also pointed out that there were plenty of native North American species that would benefit from "re-wilding" through reintroduction to parts of their historic habitats from which they had been extirpated.[12] These include the bison (*Bison bison*), pronghorn (*Antilocapra americana*), elk (*Cervus elaphus*), badger (*Taxidea taxus*), swift fox (*Vulpes velox*), various ground-dwelling squirrel species (Spermophilus spp.), and various prairie dog species (Cynomys spp.). Moreover, the puma (*Puma concolor*) is a much closer relative of the long-extinct American cheetah (*Miracinonyx trumani*) than the African cheetah. The plan's proponents had also never bothered to calculate its cost or analyzed whether the resources that would be necessary to initiate it might be better deployed elsewhere.

The Pleistocene re-wilding plan is a somewhat startling exercise of caprice, apparently motivated by its proponents' fascination with megafauna, which reflects the Northern values of the moment. The Pleistocene era was selected simply because humans are believed to have arrived in North America in that era and the proponents of this plan take a dim view of *Homo sapiens*. Worship of historical fidelity provided no guard against caprice.

and Asian) large mammals into that continent.[13] It illustrates both problems. Why the Pleistocene rather than some other era? Apparently because the proponents of the plan feel more ethically responsible for possible anthropogenic extinctions 13 000 years ago than, say, what was done to the First Nations and their homes since 1492. Why megafauna? Northern societies have long found these charismatic. The proponents of the plan seem to suggest that megafauna were more affected by anthropogenic extinctions than other taxa but any such claim does not survive serious paleoecological scrutiny. Once again, we see a cultural choice that is not easy to defend on normative grounds. Historical fidelity is no bulwark against the powers of caprice.

Leaving aside these normative worries about historical fidelity, there are other reservations as well. One is that a past system may be impossible to reconstruct given the resources available now, including the present state of a system. We will not dwell on this further, noting again that no matter what natural value we choose to enhance in a habitat we are always faced with the problem of whether it is feasible, and this will constrain what we may reasonably expect to achieve.

A more serious reservation arises from the fact that systems evolve over time. Let us say that we choose as our reference state the configuration σ_0 at time τ_0. Leave aside the question that the choice of τ_0 is arbitrary in the sense that it is a choice not dictated by ecology but, ultimately, of cultural provenance. Are we supposed to set our reference state as σ_0? The trouble is that, even without anthropogenic influence, σ_0 would have evolved into some other system today. So, perhaps, we should set as our reference state some system σ_t (where τ_t is the present time) into which σ_0 would have evolved by now. In practice this is almost always impossible to determine. For the sake of argument, let us ignore this issue. Even then, as we think more carefully about the problem, there is worse to come. Should we presume that the landscape matrix in which σ_0 was evolving was changing due to anthropogenic factors? Or not? In either case, even if we were able to determine which σ_t is appropriate, it may well be that this σ_t can only be reconstructed in the present context through highly intrusive management similar to that necessary in theme parks. Is that the purpose of restoration?

Reconstruction and Pluralism about Natural Values[14]

Recall that fidelity was only one of the natural values discussed in Chapter 2. Fidelity, of course, is not restricted to historical fidelity. We use fidelity as a criterion when we reconstruct Japanese rock gardens in north America, which are hardly part of the latter's historical past. Note that the apparently insurmountable problems faced in the last section were due to the insistence on *historical* fidelity and not fidelity in general. Suppose, for instance, the goal is just to recreate the type of wetland seen in a region. The difficulty of achieving this goal is a function of how narrowly "typical wetland" is defined. If it is defined only as a body of water—and this is intended as an extreme example—a concrete pond would suffice. If a large number of aquatic and semi-aquatic communities are specified, the problem becomes more challenging. But the practical problems are not of the same order as those encountered with historical fidelity. More importantly, the troubling normative pro-blems disappear, though we now have to provide normative justi-fication of these other values that would be used to choose a reference state (see below).

An alternative to ecological restoration (and historical fidelity) would be to embrace the full spectrum of natural values explored in Chapter 2: biodiversity, welfare, service, and wild nature, besides fidelity. As noted earlier, in contrast to the restrictive definitions discussed here, ecological restoration in practice often embraces many of these values. Two goals, directly connected to those values, have been particularly prominent in practice:

- (1) Fidelity to a regional community type, defined broadly (for instance, as discussed in the last paragraph), is often taken to be the goal. For instance, in central Texas, considerable effort is expended to create mixed oak-juniper forests (partly because this community, which is gradually decreasing in extent in this region, is supposed to provide good nesting habitat for the endangered Black-capped Vireo). There are also many attempts to "restore" tallgrass prairie on suitable soil, regardless of whether or not that particular patch of land ever was tallgrass prairie in the past.[15]

- (2) Ecosystem services that have been the target of habitat reconstruction throughout the world. Wetland restoration is commonplace. Even in the case of the Florida Everglades (Box 6.1), ecosystem services are as much the goal as fidelity to any historical past state of the system.

The first of these two goals embraces fidelity as a natural value, but not *historical* fidelity; the second embraces service (see Chapter 2 for relevant details on these natural values). Many reconstruction attempts embody both these goals and others (see, for instance, the Kristianstads Vattenrike of Sweden, described in detail in Box 7.2).

To the extent that it is appropriate to endorse the natural values discussed in Chapter 2, it also remains appropriate to pursue them in planning for the future of habitats. Which goals are the most important in a particular context depends on cultural choices. As we have already seen so many times in this book, environmental choices are cultural choices. In the context of reconstruction efforts, where humans are actively trying to plan a "new" future for a habitat, this is not a particularly surprising conclusion. It is, therefore, not surprising that some reconstruction proposals have generated a lot of controversy. Box 6.3 discusses one such recent proposal: "assisted colonization" of new habitats by species that are at high risk of extinction in their native ranges because of climate change.

A question remains, though, as to whether such efforts should all be called "restoration," given that the concept of restoration seems to suggest a return to some past state. This is where the more generic term "reconstruction" is perhaps better, but even the concept of reconstruction seems to suggest at least a partial recreation of something that already existed. Perhaps some effort should be expended in devising a name that best captures the gamut of

Box 6.3   Assisted Colonization[16]

Assisted colonization is the intentional introduction and establishment of species in sites "where they do not currently occur or have not been known to occur in recent history."[17] Assisted colonization has come to be stridently advocated— and sometimes even practiced—by a significant number of conservation biologists and environmental activists in recent years because it appears to be the best, and perhaps the only, response to the threatened extinction of many species as a result of climate change. For instance, the Florida torreya (*Torreya taxifolia*) is a conifer that is critically endangered in its tiny native range in the Florida panhandle. Only about 1000 individuals remain in the wild, with no recorded reproduction in decades. A variety of factors have contributed to the decline of this once-abundant species including disease, over-harvesting, and predation. The species is widely believed to be better adapted to climates colder than its present native range, which has led to a serious worry that climate change will inevitably lead to the Florida torreya's extinction in the wild. This prognosis has led environmental activists to try to establish a local population in the Appalachian mountains of North Carolina, more than 600 km north of the Florida torreya's known range. There is no firm evidence that shows that the species ever occurred there (though there is plenty of such speculation). Needless to say, this attempt has generated ample controversy and criticism, including objections from biologists who are sympathetic to assisted colonization but unwilling to endorse activists attempting it without professional supervision. The main criticism has always been—as in the case of any attempted assisted colonization—the risk of unforeseen consequences of such translocations including the possibility that the transplant becomes an invasive that decimates local ecological communities.

Some proponents of assisted colonization endorse translocation of species between continents but most recoil from such a policy because of the potential ecological risks associated with it—recall the discussion of Box 6.2. More credible advocates restrict translocation to sites within the same biogeographic region. Several decision-theoretic protocols (recall the discussion of Chapter 4) have been formulated, the most well-known being a decision tree that requires assisted colonization to be attempted for a species if and only if the following three criteria are satisfied:[18]

- There is a high risk of decline or extinction of the species under climate change.
- Translocation and establishment of the species is technically possible.
- Benefits of translocation outweigh biological and socio-economic costs.

All sides of the debate agree on three points: (1) Assisted colonizations will often be expensive and, given current knowledge and capacities, technically difficult. This means that at present they should only be attempted for a small suite of species. (2) Assisted colonization will typically require intrusive habitat reconstruction to ensure that transplants can prosper in their new habitats. (3) By and large, we are not concerned with species that have demand value (in the sense of Chapter 3), which are routinely translocated and managed for growth and survival because of the tangible benefits they provide.

We will return to the problem of whether the required risk analysis specified in this protocol can be credibly carried out. But, first, a suite of more fundamental ethical questions should be noted. The project of assisted colonization simply assumes that species—and not any other biological unit—are the veridical bearers of value: just the species by themselves, independent of any or all relations that they have with other entities in their present range. Now, as we saw in Chapter 5, species are often considered to be preferred constituents of biodiversity. However, in these cases, since the goal was the conservation of species in their native habitats—and not translocation—there was often a tacit assumption that the value of species arises, at least in part, from the particular relations they have with other entities in their native habitat. If this value is entirely independent of these other relations, we have a new pertinent question: why is assisted colonization preferable to preserving species in zoos and botanical gardens (or even as seeds or gametes)? Presumably any cogent answer will have to draw on some additional natural value such as wildness (recall the discussion of Chapter 2), but that will not cohere very well with the intrusive management envisioned by assisted colonization. We should also worry about how species can have such independent value. Occasionally, an appeal to transformative power (recall the discussion of Chapter 3) will suffice. However, usually, the only option will be to assign intrinsic value to species—but, now, we face all the problems with intrusive value attributions we encountered in Chapter 3.[19]

These fundamental ethical worries have not received the attention they deserve. Most criticisms of assisted colonization have come from biologists long concerned with the problem of invasive species and the history of unintended negative consequences of the introduction of non-native species almost anywhere on Earth. These biologists correctly point out that the required risk analyses can almost never be carried out in practice, especially because the full effects of these translocations may only be felt after decades and cannot be assessed in the time horizons of planning exercises.[20] Additionally, several critics have pointed out that assisted colonization, being expensive, may direct badly needed resources from traditional conservation (as in the case of re-wilding discussed in Box 6.2); moreover, it can be used as an argument against present attempts at habitat protection (see also the section "The Problem of Authenticity" in the text).

Proponents of assisted colonization have available an obvious response: restrict assisted colonization to those species for which credible risk analyses are possible, costs are acceptable, and protecting current the habitat is insufficient because of climate change. But, once these restrictions are in place, we may end up with very few species on our list for potential assisted colonization. In other words, we may be discussing a problem that only exists on paper. But it is better to discuss such decision contexts before they arise rather than after they appear and present such severe time constraints that careful decision analysis becomes impossible.

activities oriented towards the enhancement of any of the natural values from Chapter 2. Meanwhile, it is worth emphasizing that the discipline of restoration ecology, to the extent that it is dedicated to ecological restoration *sensu stricto*, does not encompass the entire range of habitat modification activities we may want to promote. Some broadening of horizons seems to be in order.

Ecological Integrity

Shifting attention to the reference dynamic, there are more problems here than plausible solutions if ecological integrity is supposed to specify what that dynamic should be. The term "integrity" was introduced into ecology through legislative fiat. Though Leopold had talked of the "integrity" of ecological communities in the 1940s, contemporary discussions of ecological integrity began with the US Federal Water Pollution Control Act Amendments of 1972, which state that their objective is to "restore and maintain the chemical, physical, and biological integrity of the Nation's waters."[21] The legislation did not define "integrity." The years that followed saw the reification of integrity into an allegedly scientific concept when managers, helped by ecologists, attempted to devise policies to carry out the legislative mandate.

In response to the legislation of 1972, in 1975 the US Environmental Protection Agency sponsored what was billed as a comprehensive symposium on the integrity of water. At the symposium, John Cairns Jr. attempted to specify and quantify integrity: "Biological integrity [is]... the maintenance of the community structure and function characteristic of a particular locale or deemed satisfactory to society."[22] Shortly afterwards, Karr and Dudley produced what has perhaps been the most influential definition of integrity. It was similar to that of Cairns but without the societal component: "the capability of supporting and maintaining a balanced, integrated, adaptive community of organisms having a species composition, diversity, and functional organization comparable to that of the natural habitat of the region."[23] (As a definition this is a bit odd since it uses the concept of integration to define integrity. In the interest of charity we will ignore this point and take the rest of the formulation to be the definition.)

There have been many variants of these definitions since their introduction, though a definitive explication of ecological integrity is yet to emerge. Given the legislative origin of the concept, this is not very surprising: there is no *a priori* reason to presume that legislative categories must seamlessly correspond to scientific concepts grounded in empirical results and the categories used to describe and organize these results.

However, the intention of the legislation and the motivation of the attempted definition are relatively clear. The crucial point is that concern for integrity forces us to look beyond the composition and structure of a system and also focus on the processes occurring within it. This is why integrity is best regarded as a dynamic criterion for the successful restoration of a system. However, there is less consensus among restoration ecologists about the role of integrity (compared to historical fidelity) as a goal of restoration. As noted earlier, the 2002 SER definition abandons integrity. While Higgs endorses it, for him it is a metaphor, though a useful one. Critics have correctly noted that the definitions offered so far remain vague and are often difficult to operationalize. However, most recent attempts to define integrity have faced the problem of operationalization squarely: proposed measures of integrity typically include both compositional parameters (what type of species, their prevalence, *etc.*) as well as hydrological parameters such as water flow that are indicative of the operation of processes.

A theme that runs through most discussions of integrity is the self-sustainability of reconstructed habitats. Cairns' definition requires the *"maintenance* of community structure and function"; Karr and Dudley speak of *"maintaining* a balanced, integrated, adaptive community of organisms" (emphasis added in both cases). Presumably, if maintenance is at such a high premium, the more easily a community is maintained the better it is. In other words, the optimal situation is when a community maintains itself; that is, when it is self-sustaining. If this chain of reasoning is correct, what is ultimately at stake is self-sustainability. Beyond restoration, in the general context of habitat reconstruction, self-sustainability may well be a more appropriate criterion for a reference dynamic than integrity. But there are other plausible options: any of the concepts of ecological stability (resilience, resistance, persistence, constancy, reliability, *etc.*) discussed in Chapter 5 may also provide reasonable candidates for what a reference dynamic should satisfy. In each case, to different extents, these stability concepts require that a system not degenerate easily by itself or in response to external influences.

Note that self-sustainability is a matter of degree, and this degree can be quantified in terms of how little external input is required to maintain the reference state and dynamics. External input may be measured in terms of the relative energy and/or biomass per unit time that has to be introduced or removed from the system. In most cases, this input would come through human agency and is, therefore, not desirable in the context of establishing self-sustainable systems. However, the extent of human intervention permissible in a successful reconstruction remains a matter of cultural choice.

The Problem of Authenticity

The question of human intervention in a natural system brings us to what is perhaps the most contentious question about environmental restoration: Should we ever intervene to alter habitats? This is not a question about whether we should intervene in natural systems to grow food or obtain building materials and other necessities of life. Obviously, we should because we must in order to survive. What is at stake is whether we can ever create "natural value" through our interventions.

Robert Elliot has argued otherwise.[24] For him the value of an entity does not only depend on the properties it has independent of all other entities; rather, it also depends on its relational properties, especially its history. (Elliot couches his discussion in terms of intrinsic values (recall Chapter 3) but that is not necessary.) According to him, the value of an entity depends in part on its genesis. Entities acquire natural value, according to Elliott, only if they evolved naturally, independent of human agency. (Note that many of the natural values that were discussed in Chapter 2 would not qualify as such under Elliot's scheme. By definitional fiat, Elliott has excluded humans from nature.[25]) As a result, a restored system lacks authenticity; its relation to the original natural system is like that of a copy to an original work of art. Elliot does not intend to denigrate all restoration efforts. If a natural system has been degraded, particularly if it has been degraded through human action, then we may even have an obligation to try to restore it. It would, in this way, acquire some value, perhaps even some natural value to the extent that what is created is independent of human control.

Elliot's main concern was to prevent people from using promises of restoration as a way of justifying natural habitat destruction. When he first introduced this argument, his immediate target was an attempt in the late 1970s to mine sand on Fraser Island, a forested sand island off the coast of Queensland in Australia. Happily for him, the Royal Commission investigating the question (the Fraser Island Environmental Commission) agreed that the natural value of the island would be irretrievably lost if mining took place, even if it was followed by meticulous restoration—Fraser Island would no longer be a "wild" place. However laudable Elliott's goal may have been, this position is based on an undefended assumption that human agency cannot generate natural value. When we look at places like Keoladeo Ghana National Park (Box 2.1),[26] is that even remotely plausible? More argument is necessary, especially when we consider within natural systems the types of human intervention that are obviously comparable to those of other species—for instance, hunting and fishing by forest-dwelling communities.

However, the problem of authenticity will not simply go away. Higgs draws attention to what is perhaps the most extreme case of the rejection of authenticity as part of what engenders natural value.[27] Higgs and Cypher explored Disney's Wilderness Lodge, a four-star hotel set in the entertainment complex of Disney World in Orlando, Florida.[28] It is designed to generate the experience of staying at one of the grand western US National Park hotels. The visitor follows Timberline Drive away from the buzz of Disney World to what appears to be a completely different realm dominated by conifer trees and an occasional redwood. The Lodge appears to be constructed of logs and is topped by a many-tiered green roof. The valet meeting guests is dressed as a park ranger. The seven-storey-high lobby appears to be encircled by wooden balconies. Rock formations reminiscent of the western United States surround the fireplace inside and dominate much of the landscape outside. Here, water seems to tumble over rocks and there even is a geyser performing more punctually than Old Faithful in Yellowstone National Park. Room interiors and furnishings are likewise consistent with what would be found in the US West around 1900. Food is similarly "authentic."

But it is all make-believe. The "logs" of the Lodge's exterior and most of the "wood" inside consist of concrete, painted with exquisite attention to detail to mimic what they are supposed to portray. The rock formations are similarly constructed and the geyser is artificial, with high-performance electronics ensuring perfect punctuality. Yet, at the perceptual level, Wilderness Lodge and its surroundings presumably provide the same sensory input as any of the sublime National Parks from the US West. But is the experience truly the same? Probably very few of us would be willing to equate the two experiences. What we value in our experiences seems obviously mediated by what knowledge we bring to them beyond the immediate input of our senses. With respect to that knowledge, in cases such as these, what seems to matter is the authenticity of an experience. In other words, we value relational properties including the historical provenance of experiences. Both Elliot and Higgs have drawn attention to an important problem: the importance of history in determining what we value and how we value it. We have more philosophical work—more reflection— ahead of us.

Notes

1. Some historical material is available Hall (2005) and Sarkar (2011) but the history of restoration ecology remains poorly explored.
2. Ecological restoration is a process or goal; in contrast, restoration ecology is a discipline with its own foundational problem. For a philosophical discussion of the latter, see Callicott (2002). This chapter focuses on the former problem, as do Higgs (2003) and Sarkar (2011).
3. See, for instance, Leopold's (1949) discussion of reclaiming land through active management.
4. See National Research Council (1992).
5. For these definitions, and those in the rest of this section, see Higgs (2003).
6. See Higgs (2003).
7. Details are from National Research Council (2003).
8. For more detail, see National Research Council (2003).
9. Presumably, very few would value the slave-holding or caste-ridden societies of the past, or the increased subjugation of women.
10. See Donlan *et al.* (2005). The initiative was loosely associated with the "Wildlands Project" of "re-wilding" North America—see Soulé and Terborgh (1999) for details of the Wildlands Project.
11. See Donlan *et al.* (2005), p. 660.
12. See Rubenstein *et al.* (2006).

13. See Donlan *et al.* (2005); for a compelling response, see Rubenstein *et al.* (2006).
14. This argument is developed in more detail in Sarkar (2011).
15. This is based on fieldwork (Sarkar, unpublished data).
16. Near-synonyms include assisted migration, assisted translocation, and managed relocation.
17. Hoegh-Guldberg *et al.* (2008), p. 345; note that, in the context of the quote, the "or" between the two criteria should be read as "and" because, if only one disjunct is true while the other is not, we would not have an assisted colonization. Nevertheless, the reference to the recent past leaves the definition underspecified even after this amendment.
18. Hoegh-Gudberg *et al.* (2009), p. 345; an alternative protocol that uses a somewhat rudimentary form of multi-criteria analysis was proposed by Richardson *et al.* (2009).
19. This problem has recently been noted by Sandler (2010).
20. See, especially, Ricciardi and Simberloff (2009).
21. See Ballentine and Guarraia (1977).
22. See Cairns Jr. (1977), p. 171.
23. See Karr and Dudley (1981), p. 55.
24. See Elliot (1997).
25. For instance, none of the ecosystem services discussed in Chapter 2 would constitute a natural value. Nor necessarily would biodiversity, for instance, if some biota are valued because of their cultural role.
26. See Sarkar (2005) for more on this example.
27. See Higgs (2003).
28. See Cypher and Higgs (1997).

7

Sustainability

The 1987 United Nations World Commission on Environment and Development (WCED), better known as the Brundtland Commission (after the Norwegian former Prime Minister, Gro Harlem Brundtland, who served as its Chair), deserves credit at least for canonizing what is perhaps the most fanciful environmental buzzword of our time: "sustainability." Chapter 2 of its report, *Our Common Future*, first defines "sustainable development" as "development that meets the needs of the present without compromising the ability of future generations to meet their needs"; and then goes on to add: "the goals of economic and social development must be defined in terms of *sustainability* in all countries—developed or developing, market-oriented or centrally planned" (emphasis added).[1] The contrast here is with economic development that leads to the exhaustion of non-renewable resources, which has been the characteristic model of development since the Industrial Revolution. (Box 7.1 describes one startling example: water extraction from ancient aquifers across the globe.)

The immediate and long-term impacts of the introduction of sustainable development as a policy goal cannot be overstated. By the time of the Rio Earth Summit of 1992 (technically, the United Nations Conference on Environment and Development), at which the Convention on Biodiversity was adopted, even biodiversity conservation had come to be seen as a component of sustainable development.[3] At least on the surface, there is conceptual

Environmental Philosophy: From Theory to Practice, First Edition. Sahotra Sarkar.
© 2012 John Wiley & Sons Inc. Published 2012 by John Wiley & Sons Inc.

**Box 7.1   Aquifer Exhaustion and Its
Consequences[2]**

Water is rapidly emerging as one of the most contested resources on Earth. Fresh water consumption rapidly increased with the growth of human populations and expansion of agriculture during the twentieth century. While the Earth's population tripled during that century, fresh water consumption went up seven-fold. Fresh water has implicitly been viewed as an infinite resource and, except in areas of known localized scarcity (for instance, deserts), there has been little effort expended on its conservation. Meanwhile access to fresh water is rapidly becoming a major issue of social justice, especially in the South, as more and more water sources are being privatized.

At present rates of consumption, by 2025, two thirds of Earth's population will face fresh water scarcity. Regions severely affected will include northern China, other large areas of Asia, as well as Africa, Australia, the US midwest, and sections of Latin America. Much of the Earth's surface water is already polluted and, increasingly, farms, cities, and industries all over the world are beginning to rely on groundwater sources for their fresh water needs. Sophisticated technology for "water mining" is being used to drill deep into the Earth's surface to extract water for daily use from ancient aquifers. Groundwater is widely recognized as a finite resource. Yet, the exponential increase of its extraction remains largely unregulated. While accurate figures are hard to obtain, it is estimated that the present rate of extraction is 750–800 km^3/year. Exactly how long reserves will last remains unknown, but in several regions groundwater depletion has already reached catastrophic levels.

For instance, groundwater in northern China is pumped at the staggering level of 30 km^3/year to provide for the needs of agriculture and industry. One consequence has been that the water table beneath Beijing has fallen by more than 20 m in the last 20 years. Drought-related sandstorms have become common, with 13 major such storms hitting northern China in just the first half of 2006. In April 2006, one of these swept across one eighth of the country, reaching Korea and Japan and dumping about 305 million kilograms of dust on Beijing alone. There are equally troubling examples from south Asia (northwest India and Pakistan, around the Indus River basin), though quantitative data are not available to an equal extent.

In other words, current fresh water use practices are not sustainable, particularly in the case of obviously finite resources such as ancient aquifers.

incoherence, if not downright dishonesty here: how is biodiversity conservation a component of sustainable *development*? As usual, *ex cathedra* pronouncements are not sufficient; at the very least, some conceptual analysis is in order. But such is the power of sustainability in contemporary environmental discourse that these questions are almost entirely ignored in policy-making contexts (though not in environmental philosophy).[4]

Though one reference to wilderness (somewhat bizarrely as an ecosystem) persisted in the Rio Convention,[5] by and large, the rhetoric of the protection of nature for its own sake had become a matter of history at least in the official international arena.[6] Over the next decade, even large transnational NGOs such as WWF and Conservation International, which had once deified wildlife at the expense of the humans who shared their habitat, changed their rhetoric to include human development as part of their brief, so long as that development was sustainable.[7] The pursuit of sustainability has even permeated everyday life in many societies: its pursuit is supposed to underpin such routine activities as reuse and recycling. It is one of the main reasons—the other being climate change—why the pursuit of renewable energy resources has emerged as a major focus in many countries of the North (and even some from the South).

What does remain to be seen is whether the concept of sustainability makes sense; that is, whether it is coherent and desirable as a policy goal. What values are embedded in the concept of sustainability? Are they all consistent? In particular, can economic development, which always requires the use of resources, ever really be sustainable? As noted earlier, the Brundtland Commission emphasizes that the concept of sustainable development contains within it two "key" concepts: "the concept of 'needs', in particular the essential needs of the world's poor, to which overriding priority should be given; and the idea of limitations imposed by the state of technology and social organization on the environment's ability to meet present and future needs."[8] The report took for granted that we had a sufficiently precise understanding of future generations' needs to carry out such an assessment; as we shall see below, that assumption is far from obvious.

Defining sustainability with care will be critical to assessing its value as a policy goal.[9] However, before we embark on that project, four basic ethical presumptions of the pursuit of sustainability should be noted:

(1) Sustainability is almost always an explicitly anthropocentric goal, referring to the interests of future *human* generations. Thus, biocentric or ecocentric concerns (recall the discussion of Chapter 3) will not necessarily be satisfied even if sustainability is attained.[10] This does not mean that sustainability is not a worthwhile goal from those perspectives. Rather, if we accept the relevance of biocentric or ecocentric goals, it means that sustainability does not exhaust all our environmental goals. Even if we endorse anthropocentrism, there still remains the possibility that the natural values we choose to promote go beyond sustainability. For instance, conserving the full spectrum of biodiversity may require more than just sustainability—we will return to this issue in some detail later in this chapter.

(2) All discussions of sustainability refer to future generations and our responsibility to them. Essentially, sustainability is about equity

towards future generations. Recall (from Chapter 3) the philosophical problems associated with demarcating obligations to individuals who do not yet exist, and whose preferences we have no way of ascertaining. All those problems must necessarily be shelved in the pursuit of sustainability. We will return to questions of intra-generational equity in the next chapter.

(3) If we are so concerned about equity towards future generations, it would be odd if we were not also willing to accept an obligation of equity towards people alive now. The Brundtland Commission explicitly addressed this issue by noting that sustainability is about development. In fact, the Commission report may be seen as an attempt at a compromise between a desire for intra-generational equity, in the form of meeting the aspirations of the South for better lives, finally, in the post-colonial era, and Northern preservationism, which argued for nature conservation in the South no matter what the human cost.

(4) Much of the discourse on sustainability simply assumes that all we are concerned with is welfare as, for instance, codified in a utility function. Some authors even see this assumption as what distinguishes *weak* from *strong sustainability* (these will be further discussed below) with the former position making this assumption and the latter rejecting it. We have seen many times in this book that utility functions may not incorporate all our values; for instance, the transformative power of experiences, as articulated in Chapter 4, which cannot be measured by felt preferences. Decision theory presumes that utility functions are all that are available to us, but that assumption, as we saw in Chapter 4, was a limitation of decision theory and responsible for some of its paradoxes. In what follows we will note the preponderance of welfare-based arguments in discussions of sustainability but will not assume that they are veridical.

Weak Sustainability

But what is *sustainability*? Robert Solow has persuasively argued that it cannot mean the conservation of all resources.[11] Consider, for example, a definition (quoted by Solow) as formulated in a UNESCO document: "every generation should leave water, air and soil resources as pure and unpolluted as when it came on earth."[12] Alternatively, "each generation should leave undiminished all the species of animals it found existing on earth." These characterizations are sometimes taken to define what is called *absurdly strong sustainability* because, at a practical level, these definitions are patently absurd. First, even without human intervention, biota change over time. These definitions seem to embody in them a particularly extreme form of the "balance of nature" mythology of unchanging ecological communities, a view that has long been discredited by ecologists, who recognize that the biosphere is far from a system in equilibrium maintained by the benevolence of some god/deity.[13] Second, it is almost certainly impossible for us to live relatively pleasant lives without diminishing some animal species sometimes. Are we not supposed to control mosquitoes carrying dengue, malaria, or yellow fever? Life without consuming some parts of our environment is biologically impossible and some of the necessary changes are probably irreversible. At the very least, we cannot have a moral obligation to do something that is not feasible. These definitions ignore this relatively obvious feature of ethical behavior.

Even more importantly, as Solow argues, policies framed using these UNESCO definitions may not even be ethically desirable: we may decide to change the Earth for our benefit (and perhaps for the benefit of future generations).[14] Our qualities of life are as improved as they are (measured, for instance, by criteria such as life expectancy) because our ancestors modified their environment (the nature around them) to make lives better for their descendants. We may choose to judge our own moral worth in terms of how much better we make the future for our descendants. Solow also persuasively argues that, if cogency is one of our desiderata, it is impossible to be excessively precise about the definition of sustainability. For him, sustainability should simply be defined as "an obligation to conduct ourselves so that we leave to the future the option or the capacity to be as well off as we are."[15] This definition is in the spirit of that of the

Brundtland Commission and avoids the problems of the UNESCO definitions.

Part of what is supposed to make precision impossible are two types of ignorance: we do not know what future generations will want or need (as was already acknowledged in Chapter 3[16]), and we do not know what will become technologically feasible. From these assumptions Solow concludes that sustainability does not require us to protect any specific resource. Rather, as is explicitly indicated in his definition, what we need to maintain is a certain capacity. As far as this capacity is concerned, Solow seems to assume that different resources are indefinitely intersubstitutable with each other (as economic goods, they are fully *fungible*). This capacity can be generated in a variety of ways, including the creation of knowledge by the present generation, which may involve the consumption of many available resources. In other words, natural resources may be substituted by human artefacts. All that sustainability requires is that the natural capital (construed abstractly, roughly, as entities that ensure continued capacity, and not as any specific resource) remains undiminished.

This position is known as *weak sustainability*: note how it draws critically on economic theory and its concept of welfare as measured by the natural capital.[17] There are many problems about whether this concept of sustainability can ever be operationalized in practical policy contexts.[18] Can we ever have such a veridical measure of natural capital? Or are we simply making in principle claims of measurability that may at best hold only for artificially simple systems? There is no easy answer to either question.

However, these practical problem pale in significance compared to more severe conceptual problems associated with Solow's argument. That argument depends critically on the ignorance assumptions. How plausible are they? We cannot entirely ignore biological constraints on our bodies. We can be as certain that the next ten generations will need air and water of a specified purity as we can be certain about any future prediction. We are less certain about how much land will be required for agriculture and we may not want to extrapolate for ten generations in this case. We can be fairly certain that emptying the Earth's aquifers (Box 7.1) will seriously restrict the options available to future generations, and in this case we can make such a claim for a specific resource. We may (happily) be wrong but it is implausible that we will have a technological solution to the problem of disposing of nuclear waste in the next generation. Deified uncertainty is a poor substitute for appropriate decisions based on reasoned judgments about future possibilities.

Moreover, as Bryan Norton has pointed out, when we talk about what is good for future generations we are not simply making a descriptive claim (as Solow seems to assume).[19] Rather we are making a normative claim about what we think are the values we should promote in society and, especially, into the future. Future preferences may depend on our choices. Recall that this is one of the reasons why responsibility to future generations is philosophically problematic (Chapter 3). However, in this case, if we are encouraging future individuals to have certain values we find desirable, our responsibility to them is presumably only enhanced.

Sustainability thus becomes a normative concept not only because we should only indulge in practices that are sustainable but also because what we take to be a sustainable society also has a normative component. If this is correct, our lack of knowledge about the preferences of future generations is at most of marginal relevance to decisions about what we should protect.

Strong Sustainability

What Norton and many other environmentalists, who often see themselves as opposed to economists such as Solow, defend is a form of *strong sustainability*.[20] This requires the protection of specific natural resources, denying the blanket intersubstitutability of resources so that only a generalized natural capital needs to be maintained. The trouble with the assumption of blanket intersubstitutability is that it is only defended by an argument from ignorance. We need not protect green plants because, who knows, we might find an equally efficient technique of sequestering the Sun's energy to sustain life on Earth. We need not maintain wildernesses because future generations may well find it equally satisfying to experience mass-produced simulations of virtual wilderness experiences. Moreover, most defenders of strong sustainability reject, in principle, the complete substitutability of natural resources by human artefacts—this is obviously related to the problem of authenticity discussed at the end of Chapter 6, with the artefactual providing less authenticity of experiences than the natural.

There are three arguments that favor strong sustainability over the weak version of the doctrine. All of them implicitly reject the force of Solow's ignorance assumptions:

(1) As noted in the last section, in some cases, we can identify specific resources that future generations must find desirable (at least insofar as they need them to survive). This is not a particularly strong argument because the number of such resources is probably relatively limited. Moreover, these resources do not include those that are usually held most dear by environmentalists; for example, biodiversity and wilderness.

(2) Unless we are using terms such as natural capital purely as metaphors, all that can be captured by the discourse of weak sustainability are those values that can be cogently captured in the concept of individual welfare and incorporated into a utility function to be potentially maximized. In this sense, weak sustainability really is no more than economic sustainability. But if we endorse goals that cannot be reduced to the pursuit of individual welfare in this way—for instance, if we endorse the normative demands that Norton defends—we must move beyond weak sustainability. To the extent that these other goals are achieved through the persistence of specific natural resources—for instance, sublime sceneries or strange or otherwise intellectually intriguing species—we need strong sustainability to have a rationale for protecting them.

(3) Most defenders of strong sustainability affirm a spectrum of natural values besides weak sustainability. Norton, for instance, advocates wilderness and old-growth forests.[21] We will develop this argument in the next section. What is really at stake here is whether sustainability should be our only policy goal or whether it should be one of many such goals. The next section will expand on a position that accepts the goal of weak sustainability where it is applicable but then advocates the pursuit of other goals, embodying other natural values. The importance of that position lies in the fact that sustainability has become so fashionable that it is often presumed to be the only environmental goal that is relevant— certainly this is the impression produced by the Brundtland Commission report and by the fact that the Rio Earth Summit even viewed biodiversity conservation as part of the pursuit of sustainable development.

The second and third arguments are related but different, though the difference between them may seem somewhat subtle. The second asserts that weak sustainability is the wrong kind of thing; the third does not make that claim but asserts, instead, that there is more to what we should want than weak sustainability.

Beyond Sustainability

An alternative position that falls somewhere between weak and strong sustainability, as conventionally understood, is one that endorses weak sustainability but assumes that there are a variety of natural values, some unrelated to sustainability, that should all be promoted. Sustainability is not the only environmental goal. Thus construed, the pursuit of sustainability does not let us abdicate our obligations to protect biodiversity, wild nature, *etc.*, even though it captures some of our natural values, for instance productivity and environmental security. In developing this position, for the rest of this section, we will assume Solow's definition of sustainability (that is, we will construe sustainability as weak sustainability).

This alternative position has two advantages: (1) It is able to take advantage of weak (or economic) sustainability in contexts in which it is appropriate. If we have a plausible plan for reversing climate change (which, incidentally, we do not), and cost-efficient renewable energy is just around the corner, it may be permissible to exhaust our fossil fuel reserves. If we invent a trivially powerful technology for desalination of sea water, it is permissible to exhaust our aquifers. However, in practice it is difficult to find such contexts. Weak sustainability may well be of vanishingly little significance in practical policy contexts.

(2) This position can easily be embedded in a broader picture of how habitats should be managed. Let us restrict our attention to terrestrial habitats. (Extension of this discussion to aquatic habitats is straightforward.) Assume that we are to plan how a landscape is to be managed, integrating all the social values that are deemed relevant. At the very least, we must set aside land (a) to protect nature, (b) for production, and (c) for habitation (as in the example from Box 5.1). Sustainability—and we need no more than weak sustainability—is critically relevant to the second and third goals ((b) and (c)). But, notice that even here it is a necessary condition but not a sufficient one. Besides satisfying our obligations to future generations, we may reasonably want to promote our own well-being as well as achieve equity in the present generation. (Recall that sustainability is shorthand for *sustainable development* but even that does not guarantee intra-generational equity). A practice could be sustainable without significantly enhancing equity beyond meeting the most basic needs of the poorest, as required by the Brundtland Commission report. Equity may put a premium on redistribution of wealth *now* that may or may not enhance sustainability.[22] Moreover, the potential for conflicts between generations is real: the pursuit of equity towards future individuals may also need more than sustainable development.) When we turn to the first goal, (a), of nature protection, sustainability is a side issue. Obviously we have to make sure that our management plans are economically viable in the long run (across generations) and, in that sense, sustainable (once again only invoking weak sustainability). But, beyond that, we could

pursue all our natural values. Interestingly, given the arguments of earlier chapters, here we do not even need to refer to future generations. We can pursue our natural values because those are our values. Future generations may well decide on different ones, even among natural values. They may reconstruct our production landscapes for their natural values but, as Solow says, it is none of our business.

Note that promoting these natural values ensures that human artefacts do not entirely replace natural resources. This position thus seems to capture much of what advocates of strong sustainability desire. (In particular, the conservation of biodiversity can be de-linked from sustainability (except in the sense endorsed in the last paragraph) and promoted independent of it.) It does so by making sustainability just one of our goals. Other goals include those natural values that are not necessarily promoted through the pursuit of sustainability. This position's main disadvantage is in the policy realm. In a world in which sustainability has become the Holy Grail of environmental policy, a plan that requires more than sustainability may find little traction. For many of its advocates sustainability has become a sufficient policy goal; here it is being viewed instead as only a necessary component of policy but not sufficient by itself. The new vision must be formulated cogently, and in more detail than attempted here. Then it must be promoted vigorously if we want to move environmental policy beyond sustainability.

Resilience[23]

In Chapter 5 we noted that "resilience," as a potential explication of stability, has been given two different definitions: (1) the rate of return of a system to its original state after a perturbation or (2) the probability of an eventual return after any perturbation. Brian Walker has recently invoked the latter definition to urge that sustainability, properly construed, consists of creating resilient social-ecological systems.[24] According to Walker and the Resilience

Alliance (a network of like-minded ecologists, resource managers, and social scientists), traditional concepts of sustainability are far too dependent on the ideal of the optimization of the procurement of goods and services: these concepts focus on efficient resource utilization as the hallmark of sustainability. But efficiency requires the removal of redundancy from a system (so as to avoid unnecessary "costs"), which typically leaves it less flexible and vulnerable to permanent change after any major disturbance. The reason is that such redundancy may permit a system to continue functioning even after one part fails because another (originally redundant one) would take over. Walker envisions such a permanent change as a transition from one regime (a set of states in which a system can be) to a radically different regime that may or may not be desirable. Problems arise when it is not.

Now, stochasticity, in the form of "random" disturbance and disruption events (such as fires, flooding, windstorms), is an ubiquitous part of the everyday world in which we live. We can choose to ignore it at our own peril. To achieve genuine sustainability—that is, the ability to persist in the current regime—Walker urges the creation of resilient systems that can recover from such stochastic events, since those events are inevitable. This will require building redundancy into systems, leading to flexibility, but with the concomitant loss of efficiency. Resilience thus helps decrease risk at the price of non-optimal efficiency. (This program is sometimes called adaptive management or adaptive governance.[25])

A system's resilience may sometimes largely depend on its ecological properties. But, because social and ecological systems are inextricably coupled in the modern world, achieving resilience may require transformation of the social system as well. Box 7.2 discusses the example of the Kristianstads Vattenrike in Sweden, in which the creation of appropriate governance mechanisms was critical for achieving resilience in a wetland habitat. The example also underscores a point made several times in this book: in the pursuit of natural values benign neglect is not an option. We must actively manage our habitats for the persistence and enhancement of natural values.

Box 7.2   Kristianstads Vattenrike, Sweden[26]

Kristianstads Vattenrike (KV) (roughly Kristianstad's "water realm") in southeastern Sweden, which covers roughly $1100\,km^2$ of the Helgeå river catchment, includes the country's largest areas of flooded meadows, traditionally used for grazing and haymaking. It provides an array of ecosystem services including the filtering of nutrients from water flowing into the Baltic Sea, recreational opportunities, and significant wildlife habitat. It was recognized as a wetland of international significance by the Ramsar Convention in 1975 and became a UNESCO Biosphere Reserve in 2005.

People have been living in the KV region for thousands of years and modifying the natural environment in a variety of ways. Since as early as the late eighteenth century there have been efforts to control the water level to benefit agriculture. On several occasions the water level was lowered in conjunction with these efforts, leading to many of the shallow lakes becoming susceptible to eutrophication. Agricultural and residential development in the 1940s increased these problems besides also polluting much of the wetland. By 1941 the city of Kristianstad had to stop obtaining its drinking water from the Helgeå river because of the pollution. Fertilizer use along the periphery of KV after World War II not only further exacerbated the threat of eutrophication but also threatened contamination of the groundwater with nitrates and biocides.

In the summer of 1964 there was a massive fish kill in the lower reaches of Helgeå river because of high organic pollution and low oxygen levels. By then, community resentment against the deterioration of the habitat had turned into outrage. Restoration attempts began in 1974 but, despite these efforts, the quality of the habitat continued to decline into the 1980s. Historical land use studies finally linked this decline to the disappearance of flooded meadows used for grazing and haymaking. Without being worked, the meadows had begun a process of ecological succession to forest and could only be reconstructed to their original form and so maintained as a cultural landscape with continued human use. In this troubled context, the Ecomuseum Kristianstads Vattenrike (EKV) emerged from local initiatives as a forum for planning and discussion for all those who were interested in restoring the KV and maintaining it as a wetland. It became the center of habitat reconstruction efforts.

A variety of local and state actors became involved in the EKV and some funding was even provided by the WWF. Eventually, the Municipality of Kristianstad assumed responsibility for running the EKV but it remained an organization that represented a variety of interests, from local to international. Most importantly, the EKV continued to serve as a forum for conflict resolution between stakeholders. The KV was made more accessible to the public and ecotourism was actively encouraged. Traditional grazing was reintroduced in some areas; mowing was introduced in others to simulate the effects of grazing. When cranes—desirable from the perspective of biodiversity and ecotourism—began to harm farmers' crops, the EKV arranged to have farmers compensated for the loss of produce in exchange for tolerating the birds.

Today, the KV is an intrusively managed landscape, a "social-ecological system," and that is the only way in which it can be sustained as a wetland. Its resilience depends on the social network responsible for its governance, representing all stakeholders and committed to flexible participatory decision making and conflict resolution.

If systems are not resilient, Walker argues, a disturbance will often initiate a transition to an entirely different regime that may not be desirable. Moreover, restoration to the original regime may become an intractable problem. According to Walker, the Florida Everglades (see Box 6.1) have already begun such a transition as cattails (*Typha* spp., mainly *T. domingensis*) have begun to take over the swampland and replace native sawgrass. The Everglades have already lost over 20 000 ha in this way, with the cattails benefiting from runoff from sugar plantations in the region. Consequently, the system's original resilience has been lost and a transition has begun to an entirely different regime. A return to the original state and its subsequent maintenance will require far-reaching structural reorganization; it will not be achieved by mere optimal management of a few system parameters. Walker does not see much hope for the current restoration efforts in the Everglades in spite of the size—and cost—of the effort. The Everglades are thus supposed to have long lost their resilience in the face of anthropogenic challenges.

Notes

1. See WCED (1987). Sustainability is also the goal of the new and fashionable program of adaptive management—this is implicit in Holling (1978) and explicit in Norton (2005).
2. Details are from Konikow and Kendy (2005) and Barlow (2007).
3. http://www.biodiv.org/doc/legal/cbd-en.pdf; last accessed 18-January-2010.
4. See, for example, Sandlund *et al.* (1992).
5. For more on this issue see Sarkar (2005), p. 38.
6. This development is particularly embedded in the rhetoric of UNESCO and other UN agencies.
7. Whether this has been done in good conscience remains debatable—see Dowie (2009).
8. WCED (1987), p. 43.
9. Holland (2001) emphasizes this point.
10. An alternative is possible. We could demand sustainability for populations of all species, in accordance with biocentrism, or become even more ambitious, in the pursuit of ecocentrism. Discussions of sustainability have rarely explored these options. Callicott and Mumford (1997) is a notable exception.
11. See Solow (1993), the *locus classicus* for a defense of weak sustainability.

12. Quoted in Solow (1993), p. 180. Somewhat strangely, this definition does not even envision the possibility that human activity could enhance these features—as, indeed, they have in much of the North over the last generation.
13. See Edgerton (1973) and Sarkar (2005, 2010b).
14. Think, for instance, of removing the scourge of vector-borne diseases or viruses such as Ebola. We have arguably already achieved this goal in the case of smallpox and it is hard to imagine that any future generation will be displeased by that choice.
15. See Solow (1993), p. 180.
16. Parfit's (1984) arguments are the most relevant ones here.
17. The distinction between weak and strong sustainability is typically traced to Daly and Cobb's (1989) much discussed work—see, for example, Norton (2005), pp. 310–316.
18. For a discussion, see Pearce *et al.* (1996).
19. This position is developed at length in Norton (2005).
20. See Norton (2005) for a development of this position, several additional distinctions between forms of strong sustainability, and a thorough exploration of related philosophical issues.
21. See Norton (2005).
22. Solow's (1993) worry about ignorance returns with a vengeance.
23. For a seminal early discussion, see Holling (1973). Folke *et al.* (2004) and Walker *et al.* (2004) provide fairly up-to-date reviews of developments since.
24. See Walker and Salt (2006) for an extensive development of these themes.
25. See Walker *et al.* (2004).
26. This case study is from Walker and Salt (2006).

8

Justice and Equity

Throughout this book we have been emphasizing the role of cultural values in framing how we describe and respond to environmental problems. If culture is relevant to our discussion, and ethics constitutes a concern, we are inevitably led to questions of justice, in particular questions about equity that have been hotly debated within many Northern and Southern environmental movements since the 1980s. This chapter will briefly examine several ideologies that have broached issues of justice as they arise in the context of addressing environmental problems. (As earlier, "ideology" is being used here to refer to wide-ranging general sets of beliefs that include a normative component; nothing pejorative is intended by the use of the term.) Each of the themes treated in this chapter (that is, each section) deserve, and have often received, book-length treatments by themselves. There is no attempt here to be comprehensive; the discussions will be limited to issues that are directly related to the rest of this book and, at best, may serve as entries to the vast related literature.

We will treat justice as being limited to humans (that is, we do not include justice towards non-human animals, other taxa, *etc.*), and we will regard justice as a necessary component of human welfare.[1] Equity is a critical component of justice: it is what we try to capture intuitively with what we call fairness. Equity is more than simply equality (see the discussion of climate change below). We will discuss both distributive justice (how environmental benefits

Environmental Philosophy: From Theory to Practice, First Edition. Sahotra Sarkar.
© 2012 John Wiley & Sons Inc. Published 2012 by John Wiley & Sons Inc.

and burdens are distributed) and procedural justice (how decisions are made).

What is perhaps distinctive about the positions discussed in this chapter is that, even when compared to the others discussed in this book, they have routinely been the basis for practice; that is, for environmental activism on the part of their adherents. In analyzing these various positions, three general ideologies are usefully distinguished. These general ideologies subsume more specific ones such as ecofeminism and social and political ecology.

(1) *Environmental fundamentalism*: Natural values trump human cultural values. If food security for impoverished villagers stands in the way of the recovery of an endangered species (say, the tiger in India, to take a well-worn example), let the people go hungry. If environmental protection requires an end to all emigration from the South to the North, so be it, even if it leads to more hunger in the South and economic near-collapse in some parts of the North; for instance, in the case of México and southern Texas. Note that, in this example, this argument against immigration is not supposed to be based on what may happen to jobs within the United States for US citizens; rather it is supposed to be based on a concern for the environment. We are also not assuming that proponents of zero immigration are closet nativists or racists. Rather, we are taking them at face value, assuming that they are genuinely motivated by environmental concerns. Does it still make you uncomfortable? Well, it probably should.

(2) *Socially responsible environmentalism*: Natural values must be negotiated with human cultural values (with this negotiation incorporating norms about both types of value). Both natural and cultural values are important. For instance, should we decide to use systematic procedures, the techniques of multi-criteria analysis (Chapter 4) can be used to make decisions that incorporate both natural and cultural values (with each criterion representing one of the values). These techniques permit different weights to be attributed to the different criteria. The extreme case would be one in which some values are held inviolable. They become what are known as hard constraints on a decision. For instance, no matter what natural

value is being promoted, we may not allow a trade-off with human life or liberty. On the other hand we may assign equal weights to creating a power station (a cultural value) and protecting a forest (a natural value) and induce a multi-criteria tradeoff between them. Most discussions of climate change and what has been called environmental racism endorse socially responsible environmentalism (see below).

(3) *Integrative biocultural environmentalism*: The central assumption of this ideology is that natural values cannot be successfully pursued without simultaneously pursuing human cultural values and *vice versa*. At first sight this seems like a wildly implausible and extreme position. Surely we can attempt to save the tiger while paying no attention to what happens to the humans sharing its habitat? There is a prudential objection: what India's Project Tiger, one of the most expensive and ambitious attempts to forestall the extinction of a single species, has shown is that conservation measures almost never work without local support.[2] Project Tiger displaced thousands of villagers without adequate, and usually without any, compensation, leaving many of them destitute. Many of these displaced villagers, quite understandably, either became poachers or entered into the service of poachers who provided them with much-needed income. Because of such prudential concerns, Dan Janzen has been emphasizing *biocultural* conservation and restoration for over 25 years.[3] But leave such prudential concerns aside. Why do we care about tigers in the first place; that is, why are they, in the terminology of Chapter 5, a *constituent* of biodiversity? As we saw there, the answer requires resort to cultural norms, what we value in nature as worth preservation. The loss of the tiger would be a debilitating cultural loss to Indians: the tiger has been one of India's most durable cultural symbols going back to the Indus Valley civilization over four thousand years ago. According to proponents of integrative biocultural environmentalism, natural values are always culturally embedded in this way. Thus, the pursuit of natural values entails the pursuit of the relevant human cultural values. The argument in the other direction is more straightforward: it reaches back to the discussion of sustainability. If human welfare requires a

sustainable relationship with nature, human welfare cannot be pursued without attention to natural values. Both social and political ecology and ecofeminism, discussed below, endorse aspects of integrative biocultural environmentalism (as does the Resilience Alliance,[4] discussed in Chapter 7).

Recall the brief discussion of deep ecology in Chapter 3. That ideology is a poster child for environmental fundamentalism. Pleistocene re-wilding (Box 6.2) is only a somewhat less apposite example. Politically, environmental fundamentalism is dangerous; for instance, when it leads to the eviction of resident peoples to create nature parks (again, recall Chapter 3 and see also the discussion of social ecology below). At the level of ethics, the problems with it are blatant: they begin with the failure to recognize that concern for the environment cannot legitimately trump all concern for human beings. This does not mean that all human concerns are legitimate. We still have to determine which of them are legitimate. But there can be no sound ethical basis for sacrificing all human interests at the altar of deified nature. We turn instead to see how the other two ideologies handle some of the perceived problems about environmental justice today.[5]

Climate Change[6]

The case of climate change is important in this context because we have to worry about the subtleties of what we take justice and equity to be rather than rely on some apparently obvious, but loose, concept of fairness. (In the other examples discussed in this chapter, many of these subtleties tend to disappear because the inequities involved are obvious.)

Let us start with some basic assumptions (which are no longer open to cogent scientific doubt). There is a continuing global anthropogenic increase of temperature resulting in part from greenhouse gas emissions, both present and past. While there is uncertainty about the extent of the future increase in temperature (see Box 4.1), even the most conservative estimates indicate the likelihood of serious negative consequences for human livelihoods (besides biodiversity). The most severe consequences will likely only be experienced by future generations but some will be felt by people alive today. If we accept future generations to be morally salient (recall the discussions of Chapter 3 and Chapter 7), we have an overwhelming responsibility to act; even otherwise, because some individuals alive today will be affected by climate change, we have some responsibility to act.

What actions are appropriate? Here there is some room for reasonable disagreement. One option is to reduce emissions. Another is to invest seriously in renewable energy technology. These are not mutually exclusive options. However, neither option is entirely free from problems. A critic of emissions reduction may claim that such reductions would do unacceptable harm to economic growth while producing negligible benefits. A skeptic about renewable energy may be just that: someone who does not believe that such technology is feasible.

Let us assume that some emissions are permissible, the exact extent to be determined through a negotiation of the disagreements noted in the last paragraph (among other concerns). How should these emissions be distributed? In a democratic decision-making context there is an obvious answer: *equally*. But, equality between what entities? Individuals? Nations? We usually take it to be obvious that the answer should be the latter, but that is only because policies about issues such as climate are typically made by nation states in our age. (This may change, for instance, if some of these decisions are abrogated to transnational bodies such as the European Union.) But, even then, there remains a morally salient question: why should all nations be treated as equal irrespective of their populations, economic status, and history?

Most importantly, a single nation, the United States, is responsible for 20 percent of all emissions (which total 26 billion metric tons each year). Another, China, contributes another 15 percent, with the nations of the European Union jointly adding another 14 percent. If we look at *per capita* carbon emissions, China's contribution is much lower. The United States contributes about 20 metric tons of carbon per person per year, China contributes less than 4 metric tons, while Russia contributes about 10 metric tons and India a little more than one metric ton. Over 60 countries contribute less than one metric ton per person. For some countries there is no measurable emission at all.

If we look at historical patterns, we see similar discrepancies in cumulative emissions with the United States again responsible for about 30 percent of the emissions between 1850 and 2002, with the nations of the European Union jointly contributing about 36.5 percent and Russia contributing about 8.1 percent. Since 1850 the North has been responsible for 76 percent of carbon dioxide emissions; the South, including huge countries such as China and India, has been responsible only for the other 24 percent.

Distributing emission reductions equally between all nations no longer seems morally appropriate. This conclusion is reinforced when we realize that the same (absolute or relative) decrease of emissions would affect individuals in different nations differently. What would be a matter of subsistence in Bangladesh may well be a matter of luxury in the United States. The conclusion to be drawn is that equality may be trumped by other morally relevant considerations.

In a penetrating discussion of the ethics of climate change, James Garvey suggests four criteria of moral adequacy to replace simple equality:[7] (1) historical responsibilities, (2) present capacities, (3) sustainability, and (4) procedural fairness. All four are relevant to equity. Historical responsibilities, in this case past emissions, impose a greater burden of emission reduction on nations of the North than those of the South. Present capacities impose the same requirement both because of the disparity of current emissions and because of the disproportionate effects of the same reduction in nations of the North and the South. These computations can be made either using aggregate national or *per capita* statistics; given the huge variation in national populations, using the latter is more consistent with democratic intuitions, which regard all individuals on par with each other. Qualitatively, the conclusions remain the same. Sustainability is a matter of equity for future generations—recall the discussions of

Chapter 7. Those who consume more obviously can and should do more to achieve sustainability, both locally and globally. Northern patterns of over-consumption make nations of the North more liable than those of the South. Once again, qualitatively, it does not matter whether we use national or *per capita* statistics in spite of the much higher population of the South (which includes China and India). Finally, procedural fairness requires that all parties have access to all the relevant information and fully participate in decision-making processes so that consent is genuine. (This is part of participatory justice.) It may seem trivial but participants from the South have routinely been under-represented in environmental decisions. When these adequacy criteria are deployed to characterize equity, in place of naive equality, there is no question that the responsibility for acting on climate change belongs today primarily to the nations of the North.

Environmental Racism[8]

The South will experience a disproportionally higher share of the negative effects of climate change than the North both because of its higher populations and because it has less resources to cope with climate change than the North. By and large, the South consists of people of color and most Northerners are white. Given that climate change is largely anthropogenic, and its extent is now a matter of our conscious choice, there is no question that basic principles of distributive justice are being called into question by such consequences of climate change. But is this phenomenon indicative of *racism*? The answer is not trivial. Not all discrimination is racial. Moreover, for any form of discrimination, we must distinguish between *intent* and *effect*. If (morally unsupportable) discrimination is intentional, blame is easy. If all we can see are discriminatory effects of some policy that is not explicitly intended to discriminate in this way, then the situation is more complex. (We are assuming, for the sake of this argument, that we have no reason to question the honesty of reported intentions. In practice, we would have to be very gullible to make such an assumption when faced with blatant discriminatory effects.) Discrimination may be individual but it may also be institutional, as we have learned in the cases of race and gender throughout the world. Social structures such as old boys' clubs may have been set up with no conscious discriminatory intent but may, nevertheless, result in morally culpable discrimination, for instance on the basis of race or gender. A slightly less extreme example is many golf clubs in the United States. In such situations effect is enough to assign moral responsibility—and, often enough, legal culpability, as courts in the United States usually accept.

From slavery through segregation to the civil rights movement, given the racial history of the United States, it is not surprising that the question of racism has been debated in the US environmental movement with respect to both the distribution of environmental benefits and burdens as well as participation in environmental decisions. That debate began in earnest in the early 1980s in the community of Afton in Warren County, North Carolina. In 1980, Afton was 84 percent African-American and Warren County had the largest proportion of African-Americans among the counties of North Carolina. Unemployment in Warren County was 13.3 percent, the second highest in North Carolina. In 1982, Charles E. Cobb, a director of the United Church of Christ's Commission for Racial Justice (UCC-CRJ) began criticizing the Warren County PCB Landfill for disproportionately affecting African-Americans and the poor.[9] (PCBs (polycholrinated biphenyls) are highly toxic organic compounds, once used by the electrical industry, which bioaccumulate in animals including humans. Their production was banned in most US counties in the 1970s.) Cobb's criticism let to a non-violent civil disobedience campaign that included a blockage of trucks transporting PCB-laced soil and that resulted in over 500 arrests.

While the campaign was unsuccessful in stopping the landfill, it made the US General Accounting Office conduct a study of hazardous waste landfill siting. This study, published in 1983, found a strong correlation between the presence of such sites and the race and socio-economic status of nearby communities. A subsequent national study by UCC-CRJ confirmed these conclusions: "Race proved to be the most significant among variables tested in association with the location of commercial hazardous waste facilities."[10] The UCC-CRJ report was the first to explicitly mention environmental *racism*; subsequently it was defined by Robert Bullard as "any policy, practice, or directive that differentially affects or disadvantages, whether intended or unintended, groups or communities based on race."[11] It is implicit in this definition—and explicit in the context in which it was offered—that the reference is to policies that have environmental impacts whether or not they were motivated by environmental concerns. Thus, this definition is based entirely on the effect of a policy, ignoring its intent. If this definition is accepted, there is little doubt that environmental racism is widespread, at least in the United States.

But there is room for caution. It may well be that environmental problems are in general more often encountered by those who are economically disadvantaged because these people have less political power. The association with race may then result from a correlation between race and poverty. In philosophical jargon, a racial discrimination effect and environmental harm may have a common cause: poverty. In any case, talk of poverty and environmental harm takes us seamlessly to social and political ecology.

Social and Political Ecology

In the 1980s, Ramachandra Guha's critique of deep ecology and wilderness preservationism probably marked the first time that the North became aware of a distinctively Southern ideology of social ecology.[12] Guha traced this ideology back to work by Indian sociologists from the 1940s. Guha's critique had both a negative agenda and a positive program. The negative agenda had two parts. One was the criticism of environmental fundamentalism that has already figured prominently in this book and need not detain us any further. The other was a critique of Northern claims that environmentalism was a "post-material" concern that individuals indulged in (a "luxury good" in a post-material society) only when material needs were satisfied. In response, social ecologists pointed out that the poor, especially in the South, depended unavoidably on resources extracted directly from nature, for instance food, water, and home-building materials. It requires some imagination to regard these materials as post-material luxury goods and, at least to that extent, it is hard to disagree with the criticisms directed by social ecologists against the post-materialist thesis. (Some social ecologists explicitly referred to their agenda as the environmentalism of the poor.[13])

Turning to the positive program, concern for justice, implicitly distributive justice, dominated the goals of social ecology. The positive program included the advocacy of a framework in which social and ecological processes would be simultaneously modeled. (Here, social ecology has quite remarkable similarities to the agenda of the Resilience Alliance discussed in Chapter 7.[14]) Biocultural integration was to be achieved through science, but science was to be deployed as a tool for social justice. In practice, social ecologists produced few quantitative analyses even though at least some of them held that goal to be an important component of their program. However, the conceptual models they produced were integrative in the sense that natural and cultural goals were not necessarily distinguished before all goals were potentially traded off against each other.[15] Ultimately, the most valuable theoretical contribution of social ecology, so far, may well have been its negative critique rather than the positive program.

Its practical contributions are easier to enumerate. These include the Chipko movement in the north Indian Himalayas (Box 8.1), and the struggle of rubber tappers in the Brazilian Amazon and of the Ogoni people in the Niger delta of Nigeria.[17] Even here it is doubtful, though, that the activists within these movements perceived themselves as social ecologists. Rather, the connection they saw between maintaining natural values and their own material well-being was one of the foundational assumptions of social

Box 8.1 The Chipko Movement[16]

The Chipko movement emerged in the Indian Himalayas in the 1970s when local peasants, mainly women, acted to prevent deforestation by timber contractors authorized by the Uttar Pradesh State Forest Department. Local residents correctly posited a causal connection between deforestation, subsequent erosion, and a devastating flood in 1970, accompanied by landslides, which killed a large number of people and cattle besides destroying much property and most of the local communications infrastructure. Equally at stake was the control of forest resources including timber and resin, on which local economies were critically dependent, as well as access to developmental resources, which were unequally distributed. Later, the focus of some participants expanded to include opposition to mining and hydroelectric projects because they also destroyed forests.

Protests began in earnest in 1973 with the first successful resistance to forest felling taking place in the Mandal forests; the main immediate demand was a higher allotment of trees for felling to a local organization instead of outside loggers contracted by the Forest Department. The movement came to be called "*chipko*" (which means "to adhere" or "to stick to") because activists were supposed to have hugged trees to prevent them from being felled by loggers. It reached a high point in 1974 when a group of women in the Reni forests, led by Gaura Devi, the head of the local village women's organization, succeeded in physically chasing away the timber contractors. A large majority of the activists were women because women were more directly affected by the deforestation: they gathered fodder, fuel, *etc.* from the forests while men were often working or seeking jobs elsewhere. The leadership emphasized "five Fs" as demands: food, fodder, fuel, fertilizer, and fiber. However, the movement always remained multi-faceted, with different groups having different emphases. Part of the explanation for its success is that no centralized structure attempted to impose authority over local initiatives.

When negotiations between villagers and the State Forest Department reached an impasse, some of the movement's leaders, including Sundarlal Bahaguna, appealed for intervention from the federal Indian government. Through clever use of rhetoric and media attention, the movement managed to garner extensive national and international attention and support. Though the Indian federal government did not immediately intervene directly, its endorsement of the movement pressured the State government to enact legislation in 1976 to address many of the movement's grievances, including providing substantial local control of forest resources. In 1976 the federal government also introduced a constitutional amendment that banned large-scale deforestation anywhere in the country without its express consent. Nevertheless, the apparent success of the movement remains subject to reinterpretation: the ban on logging and other measures largely stopped local economic development, which was one of the original demands of the movement's participants. Economic development later became a central goal of the Uttaranchal movement, which succeeded in seceding from Uttar Pradesh as a separate state in the Indian union and included the Chipko areas.

ecology and, to that extent, these movements naturally fall under the rubric of this ideology. But it does not prevent other ideologies from also claiming these movements (see, for instance, the discussion of ecofeminism below). No final assessment of social ecology can ignore the successes and failures of these movements—but that is beyond the scope of a philosophy book (besides it being perhaps yet a little too early to pass such historical judgment).

What is designated as political ecology—and the term subsumes a wide variety of practices that are being lumped together here—in the North has many similarities to the social ecology of the South, and it is questionable whether the two disciplines are usefully distinguished, especially given that some authors such as Joan Martinez-Alier straddle both disciplines.[18] Political ecology emerged as a recognizable discipline in the 1970s partly as a response to the neglect of political analysis in human ecology and ecological anthropology. A particular target was the growing popularity of naive human sociobiological explanations of human social structures, which attempted to reduce these features to genes that were favored by natural selection. Ultimately, these explanation were no more than just-so stories about evolutionary adaptation.[19]

A wide variety of disciplines contributed to the development of political ecology including, most notably, anthropology, geography, and political science. A seminal early contribution was Piers Blaikie's analysis of soil erosion in the South, which was persuasively interpreted as resulting from land appropriation policies rather than overexploitation by naive farmers (see Box 8.2 for the example of Niger).[22]

Given the wide variety of analyses that are subsumed under political ecology, the discipline resists succinct definition. As the first editors of the *Journal of Political Ecology* put it: "As semi-devout Wittgensteinians, we feel it would be ill-advised to define 'political ecology' and maintain rather that all legitimate forms of political ecology will have some family resemblances but need not share a common core."[23] Nevertheless, two themes have been dominant in the practice of political ecology: (1) an analysis of social power relations and their effects on daily life and productivity and (2) the mutual dependence of these relations on the environmental substrate of a community. The example in Box 8.2 underscores what is philosophically important in political ecology: its refusal to commit exclusively to either ecological or political causes of environmental change, its commitment to the analysis of social power relations, and its emphasis on contextual detail.

Box 8.2   Causes of Soil Erosion in Niger

Landlocked Niger, with much of its area in the Sahel region just south of the Sahara desert, experienced a famine between 1968 and 1974 that led to thousands of human deaths, livestock depletion by about half, ruin of most of the agricultural crops, and violent conflict between (mainly Fulani) herders and farmers. During that period sub-Saharan Africa became a net food importer even though it had traditionally been an exporter of agricultural goods, including food. Crop yield per hectare declined in spite of fairly sophisticated attempts at technological solution. Meanwhile, wind erosion degraded barren soil on both farms and pastures. The crisis persisted into the 1980s. Academic analyses by international experts blamed overpopulation and industrial backwardness. However, an analysis by an anthropologist, Richard Franke, and a sociologist, Barbara Chasin, produced a different answer: peanuts.[20] This analysis was one of the first definitive contributions that led to the formation of political ecology as an identifiable academic discipline

Franke and Chasin's causal analysis is shown in Figure 8.1. Peanut farming (one of the two causal sources, shaded light gray, in Figure 8.1) had been introduced in the nineteenth century by French colonial administrators and championed by those who succeeded them after Niger's independence in 1960. The expectation was that peanut oil, produced in Europe, would compete well in the international market (especially against north American soybean crop) and would generate export income for Niger while providing cheap supplies to European processors.

The trouble is that the policy did not take account of the local biological ecology of the region (see Figure 8.1), let alone the social ecology of human livelihoods. Moreover, global oil markets dictated the price of peanuts, and inflated prices initially paid to farmers through subsidies declined

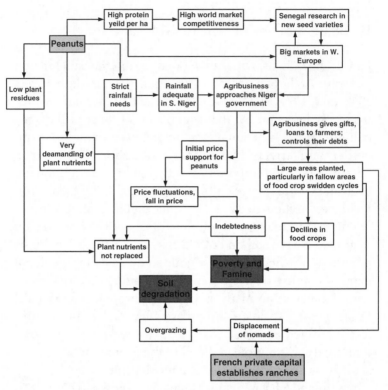

Figure 8.1 Peanuts, poverty, and soil erosion in Niger. The causal network is presented as a directed graph with arrows indicating causal influent. Source vertices are shaded light gray; sinks are shaded dark gray.[21]

by 22 percent in the decade after independence, just before the drought hit the region. Meanwhile, in 1970, 65 percent of Niger's export income came entirely from peanuts. The drought displaced herders, a process exacerbated by French (colonial and post-colonial) expropriation of land traditionally used by the Fulani to create "ranches" (the other light gray source box in Figure 8.1). Even before that, the Fulani had already been deprived of much of their grazing land because of the expansion of peanut agriculture.

The causal network of Figure 8.1, including the effects of planting in a region traditionally left fallow in a swidden cycle, is easy to follow. The network ends in the dark gray red boxes of soil erosion and poverty and famine. What is critical is that poor technology and overpopulation are not the light gray originators of the problem. In fact, they do not even emerge as causal players in Figure 8.1. For political ecologists the conclusion is obvious: if we look for the most salient causes of soil erosion (and poverty and famine) in Niger in the 1970s, the standard Northern answers of overpopulation and technological backwardness are incorrect.

Once we dig deeper in the pursuit of the drivers of erosion and poverty, political arrangements are what matter. There are fairly obvious issues of equity and justice, though they are sometimes subtle. With the case of the displacement of the Fulani from their traditional grounds, the issues are not that subtle. But when it comes to incentives and subsequently subsidies that disappear—and no local understanding that this may happen—the questions are similar to those about informed consent in medical ethics.

All of these themes are equally pertinent to social ecology. However, the analyses that emerge from the two disciplines tend to differ somewhat in emphasis. Political ecology tends to focus on social power relations whereas social ecology generally focuses on environmental resource constraints and opportunities. Moreover, perhaps because of social ecology's origins in Southern contexts, its proponents are more often directly engaged in environmental activism than their political ecologist counterparts, who are usually from the North and often play a largely academic role of interpreting such practice rather than engaging in it. This is a coarse-grained generalization and exceptions are easy to find. The commonalities between social and political ecology that were noted earlier are much more pertinent than the differences.

Ecofeminism

It will not be possible to do justice to the rich literature of ecofeminism in the few paragraphs that are devoted to it here.[24] It may even have been wiser to eschew any discussion of the topic altogether, leaving it for a different work, given that any such short treatment is bound to suffer at least from errors of omission and over-simplification. Nevertheless, leaving it out altogether would result in an equally egregious problem, suggesting that ecofeminism has not made any serious contribution to environmental philosophy. The discussion below will leave out variants of ecofeminism, which are also worth attention. Nevertheless, we pick what seems to be the lesser of two evils by paying some attention to the discipline.

Ecofeminism emerged in the 1970s when feminists began postulating theoretical connections between sexism and the domination of nature. If there is any single claim that is common to the wide diversity of ecofeminist positions, it is that there is a connection between the domination of women by men and the domination of nature by humans. Neither can be addressed without the other: this is the sense in which ecofeminism also exemplifies integrative biocultural environmentalism.

The intellectual force of ecofeminism ultimately depends on the status of the postulated connection between the domination of women and the domination of nature. For the purpose of the discussion of ecofeminism we will assume that the domination of nature is morally salient (and undesirable). This assumption does not cohere comfortably with the rest of this book, which attempts to incorporate a more nuanced view of the human role in the rest of nature. However, without this assumption, we would lose what is distinctive about ecofeminism, which requires both this assumption and the postulated connection between the domination of women and the domination of nature. Suppose that we were to only recognize the moral salience of the domination of women and not that of the domination of nature. We could still act on the this moral judgment. However, such action could easily be motivated by social or political ecology; it would not require ecofeminism. Both assumptions, the moral critique of nature domination and its connection to the domination of women, are critical to ecofeminist arguments.

But the connection between the domination of women and the domination of nature requires elaboration and argument. Some ecofeminists have attempted to establish the connection by drawing on history. Box 8.3 describes one such attempt that traces both modes

Box 8.3 The Feminist Critique of the Scientific Revolution

Carolyn Merchant has argued that the transition from an "organic" to a "mechanistic" metaphysics during the Scientific Revolution (from the fifteenth to the seventeenth centuries) led to a devaluation of both women and nature.[25] This devaluation was partly a consequence of the shift from an Earth-centered view of the universe to a Sun-centered one. In the medieval worldview, the Earth was supposed to be associated with two aspects of womanliness: the nurturing mother and the potentially violent and chaotic uncontrollable female. In contrast, the Sun was associated with manliness. Merchant quotes Copernicus: "the earth conceives by the sun and becomes pregnant with animal offspring."[26] According to Merchant, the fact that change could occur in the heavens, and not only on Earth, led to a fear that nature's order could break down. This is supposed to be the source of the desire to control nature, which was undeniably a part of the Scientific Revolution. Since the control of nature was the motivation, the aspect of womanliness that came to be associated with nature was that of the violent and chaotic female. In support, Merchant quotes Francis Bacon, writing to his mentor, James I of England:

> For you have but to follow and hound nature ... and you will
> be able to lead and drive her afterward to the same place
> again.... Neither ought a man to make a scruple of entering
> and penetrating those holes and corners, when the inquisition
> of truth is his whole object—as your majesty has shown in his
> own example.[27]
>
> James I was a strong supporter of witch hunts and trials, and
> Bacon was finding what was for him an apt analogy between
> nature and a woman being tried for witchcraft with her body
> being indiscriminately violated. For Merchant, the increased
> oppression of women in this period was partly a result of
> increased visibility, for instance, due to their participation in
> the Protestant movements of northern Europe and because of
> the long reign of Elizabeth I in England.

of domination back to the Scientific Revolution, which is supposed to
have introduced both of them.[28] The plausibility of this argument
depends on whether we are willing to accept, especially in the
European context, that the status of women was less oppressive
before the Scientific Revolution than after the Enlightenment. Most
historical excavations suggest otherwise though the issue remains
open to interpretive debate.

But there are other lines of argument. Val Plumwood attempts to
establish the connection through an analysis of what she views as a
series of related "dualisms" in Northern cultures: cultural constructs
by which differences between two entities are viewed as making
them oppositional, mutually exclusive, with one dominating
the other, and with this domination viewed as morally salient.[29]
The human/nature and mental/manual are two such distinctions, in
both cases with the first member of the pair deemed to be morally
superior to the second. Another such distinction is the masculine/
feminine. The point is that these dualisms are not veridical; rather,
they are constructs imposed by oppressive social structures. Implicitly, what is being postulated is some sort of ontologically relevant

connection between the dominant member of each such pair and, similarly, between each dominated member. Thus, paying attention to feminist concerns results in an attention to nature and *vice versa*. The trouble is that there is no sense in which the masculine/feminine emerges as the privileged dualism from this analysis. We may as well start with the mental/manual, which may lead to what used to be called vulgar Marxism. This point is important because, unless we can privilege the masculine/feminine pair, we would not be doing eco*feminism*.

Yet another argument comes from a postulated "logic of domination." Humans as sentient beings are supposed to be superior to, say, plants (with sentience being the indicator of this superiority). Thus humans are entitled to subordinate plants. Now, identify humans with the mental and women with nature and, ultimately, with plants or other non-sentient beings. It follows that society (humans) is entitled to subordinate women. Now, whatever that is flawed with this line of argument is supposed to be relevant in both instances of the logic of domination. Thus, feminist activism would lead to a more just relationship with nature. The trouble, once again, is that there is no argument as yet that privileges the feminist basis. One could just as well start with environmental fundamentalism and argue that resolving issues about the domination of nature will liberate women.

For some feminists, the required privilege for the feminist basis is obtained by assuming what is called a standpoint epistemology. Women have epistemic privilege simply because they have experiences that are distinctive to women. Though it remains unclear whether this privilege is the result of biology, socialization, or both, the privilege is enough to underpin the arguments of the last two paragraphs (that is, to provide the required privileging of the feminist standpoint). Some ecofeminists such as Vandana Shiva take this further and, even among women, give additional privilege to the South. Shiva writes:[30]

In contemporary times, Third World Women, whose minds have not yet been dispossessed or colonized, are in a privileged position to

make visible the invisible oppositional categories that they are cus-
todians of.... Third World women and those tribals and peasants
who have been left out of the process of maldevelopment, are today
acting as the intellectual gene pools of ecological categories of thought
and action. Marginalization has thus become a source for healing the
diseased mainstream of patriarchical development.

Needless to say, other ecofeminists, such as Victoria Davion,
remain unconvinced by such claims. They demand, at the very
least, coherent argument in place of *ex cathedra* pronouncements
such as the ones contained in the passage from Shiva quoted above.
This is a debate within ecofeminism. However, it is probably uncontroversial to say that the question of privileging remains a
problem for that discipline. But the political consequences of
ecofeminist practice are tangible: the Chipko movement (Box 8.1),
led by women, is sometimes interpreted as an exemplar of
ecofeminist activism.

Notes

1. For lack of space, and consistent with the rest of this book, issues
   connected to animal rights, *etc.*, are being ignored. Aaltola (2009) is an
   introduction to that literature.
2. For more on this example, see Guha (1989a) and Agarwal (1992).
3. See Janzen (1986), which was an important early realization of the
   interpenetration of cultural and natural goals in biodiversity
   conservation.
4. See Walker and Salt (2006); however, there is little explicit discussion of
   norms in the work of the Resilience Alliance.
5. For general overviews of environmental justice discussions, see
   Figueroa and Mills (2001) and Figueroa (2009).
6. Garvey (2008) and Jamieson (2009) provide an entry into the literature.
7. See Garvey (2008). The numbers reported in this section are from that
   source.
8. Details are from Figueroa and Mills (2001) and Figueroa (2009), which
   provide the relevant sources for the case studies.
9. See United Church of Christ Commission for Racial Justice (1987).

10. United Church of Christ's Commission for Racial Justice, p. xiii.
11. See United States House of Representatives (1993), p. 47.
12. See Guha (1989a). Social ecology, as discussed in this chapter, is a Southern ideology originating in India. The crucial texts are collected by Guha (1994). In north America, "social ecology" is often used to describe a rather different ideology associated with Murray Bookchin (1995)—see the review by Crist (2009). The two uses of "social ecology" should not be conflated.
13. See, for instance, Martinez-Alier (2002).
14. See Walker and Salt (2006), which, however, eschews discussion of norms.
15. See, for example, Sarkar and Montoya (2010), who analyze the case of Kandozi activism and resource conservation decisions in Perú and also try to establish connections between social ecology and systematic conservation planning (as described in Table 5.1).
16. Most details are from Guha (1989b); Rangan (2000) provides a variant interpretation of the same developments.
17. See Guha (1989b) and Rangan (2000) for the Chipko movement; Revkin (1990) for material on the rubber-trappers of the Brazilian Amazon; and Okonta and Douglas (2003) for the Ogoni struggle.
18. See Martinez-Alier (2002); there has been surprisingly little explicit discussion of the relationships between the two ideologies.
19. For detailed criticisms of these explanations, see Gould and Lewontin (1979) and Lewontin *et al.* (1984).
20. See Franke and Chasin (1981).
21. Redrawn from Franke and Chasin (1981).
22. See Blaikie (1985).
23. See Greenberg and Park (1994).
24. Davion (2001) and Warren (2009) provide useful entries into this literature.
25. This theme is most extensively developed in Merchant (1983). All quotations are from that source.
26. Merchant (1983), p. 16.
27. Merchant (1983), p. 168.
28. See Merchant (1983), though this theme does not occur in many recent reviews of ecofeminism—see, for instance, Warren (2009).
29. See Plumwood (1993).
30. See Shiva (1990), p. 190; for the response, see Davion (2001).

9

Where Does This Leave Us?

What does philosophy contribute to the solution of the problems that spawned the rise of what has been called environmentalism since the last quarter of the twentieth century? Directly, perhaps, its contribution is primarily through decision theory (Chapter 4) and, especially, through the analysis of moral responsibility for climate change (Chapter 8). In both cases, philosophy enters into how we translate ethics into public policy. The paradoxes of decision theory show that not all our intuitions about good decisions in the public sphere can be simultaneously satisfied. When there are multiple conflicting objectives, decision theory provides tools for synthesizing these objectives to the extent possible, incorporating trade-offs where necessary. When different agents have different agendas, for instance in group negotiations, in many context, conceptual difficulties associated with aggregating preferences may indicate that a deliberative process would be better than mechanical aggregation. These insights from decision theory are not limited to environmental contexts; they are equally applicable in all other policy contexts. Nevertheless, compared to many other such contexts, decision theory has more often been ignored in environmental decision making and may thus have even more to contribute here than in those other contexts.

Perhaps equally importantly, philosophy encourages critical thinking about deeply held but unexamined beliefs. Take one example from Chapter 3. Environmentalists, particularly in north

Environmental Philosophy: From Theory to Practice, First Edition. Sahotra Sarkar.
© 2012 John Wiley & Sons Inc. Published 2012 by John Wiley & Sons Inc.

America, are prone to attribute intrinsic value to environmental features. Recognition of the intrinsic value of nature, rather than the pursuit of human values, is supposed to underpin a genuinely ethical attitude to the environment. Intrinsic value attributions may well help us extend our moral considerations to other sentient beings and prevent us, for instance, from farming animals with extraordinary cruelty or killing them simply because of our vanity about how we dress. But these attributions are also supposed to provide a normative basis for the conservation of biodiversity. The discussions of Chapter 3 suggest that finding such a basis from intrinsic value attributions will not be easy, if at all possible.

In fact, some members of a working group from the US National Center for Ecological Analysis and Synthesis that included an unusual number of professional philosophers have recently argued that intrinsic value attributions provide a poor guide for biodiversity conservation policy once we adopt the framework of decision theory to bridge the gap between ethics and public policy.[1] Basically, the argument is that intrinsic values cannot be incorporated into a utility function that is maximized in optimal decisions.

But this argument is far from definitive. As Baird Callicott points out, in a democratic society we routinely reason about things that we do not explicitly incorporate into utility functions or evaluate using market mechanisms.[2] We still make policies about them. For example, we make policies to protect individual liberty, regulate sexual behavior, and give special status to places of worship. We have even developed methodologies to quantify reparations when such policies are violated without having to attribute monetary values to the entities themselves. A civil court may determine compensation for a wrongful death and even award punitive damages without getting into the business of ascribing a monetary value to life itself.[3] This is an argument amongst philosophers—its importance to those who are not philosophers is to demonstrate the complexity of intrinsic value attributions in environmental contexts.

In any case, rather than summarily dismiss intrinsic value attributions, it may be wise to explore, even if we can only speculate, what motivates those who see force in these attributions. At least in part,

197

the motivation probably comes from the sense that we demean nature if we judge its value by what it contributes to us. For this book, the question then becomes whether the attribution of transformative power meets this challenge. After all, the experiences that are presumed to have transformative power change how we view the world and, because of that, are probably among the most important experiences that we ever have. Is nature still being demeaned when this type of power is being attributed to our experiences of biodiversity, wilderness, *etc.*?

Recourse to transformative power is also how Chapter 3 accounted for our reverence towards important human artefacts such as historical monuments and works of art. In other words, the account of transformative power is ambitious enough to try to be a general theory of aesthetics that encompasses both the cultural and the natural. Does it work? At the very least, the challenges of the boundary and directional problems (Table 3.2) must be met. There is much more work to be done.

The discussions of several chapters, particularly Chapters 2 and 6, also suggest that we need a much deeper understanding of the ways in which we value nature and how it contributes to our well-being. The inventory of natural values in Chapter 2 is no more than a cursory first pass. What is surprising is how little attention has been paid to this issue. As noted in Chapter 6, natural values have probably been pursued at least since human beings began settled agriculture and manipulated their surroundings to enhance productivity. The ancient civilizations of Mesopotamia celebrated their gardens. In India there are records of forest management dating back at least to four centuries before the common era. The massive anthropogenic modification of habitats since the Industrial Revolution has made the active pursuit of natural values more important than ever before: mere preservation of natural values by conservation of habitats is not enough. Does the inventory of Chapter 2 exhaust these natural values? How are the various natural values related to each other? Which are appropriate in what contexts? What we still lack is a rich discussion of natural values comparable to the voluminous work on the aesthetics of human artefacts. Philosophy may have much to contribute towards establishing an understanding of natural values.

In this context, a perhaps somewhat unexpected conclusion to be drawn from the discussions of earlier chapters is the remarkable extent to which cultural norms play an unavoidable role in how we conceptualize environmental goals, both in how we frame problems and what we judge to be acceptable solutions. Cultural values were central to the definition of biodiversity (Chapter 5). They are obviously equally central to habitat reconstruction, including ecological restoration (Chapter 6). They are also relevant to discussions of sustainability, whether weak sustainability is enough, and whether strong sustainability is better replaced with a platform endorsing weak sustainability and an array of goals embodying natural values not captured by weak sustainability (Chapter 7).

Perhaps the take-home message for environmental activists is that the future they envision can only be achieved if natural values are embedded into the cultural fabric of a region. The biologist and pioneer advocate of biocultural conservation Dan Janzen realized this over 20 years ago when he argued: "Within the next 10–30 years (depending on where you are), whatever tropical nature has not become embedded in the cultural consciousness of local and distant societies will be obliterated to make way for biological machines that produce physical goods for direct human consumption."[4] What Janzen notes about the tropics is equally applicable elsewhere. Natural values are cultural values: the problem is to get societies to appreciate natural values as part of what makes life worthwhile.

Embracing culture lets us seamlessly integrate social goals of equity and justice into our thinking about environmental issues. As we saw in Chapter 7, sustainability is about equity towards future generations. In Chapter 8 we returned to the present generation. Except for environmental fundamentalism, the other ideologies mentioned there all merit exploration but, perhaps, social and political ecology deserves even more attention from activists than the others. What these disciplines remind us is that, when we search for explanations of complex natural and social phenomena, we should not *a priori* exclude categories of explanation, in particular those that embrace institutionalized structures. Rather we should be constantly aware of the interpenetration of social and cultural factors to form composite ecological systems. Further, both the cultural and ecological histories of a region matter, and local idiosyncratic detail may well prove to be the most salient factor in an explanation. Without detailed analysis, who would have thought that peanuts were connected to soil erosion in the Sahel (Box 8.3)? Above all, social and political ecology warns us of the danger of glib Northern explanations of problems in the South, such as overpopulation and technological backwardness.

Discussions of social and political ecology take us back to a fundamental philosophical problem. Behind many of the discussions of environmental philosophy—and perhaps most of the controversies in environmental ethics—is an issue that, though already broached several times in this book (especially in Chapter 2), nevertheless deserves reiteration. Are humans separate from nature? From the perspective of biology, obviously we are not. Nevertheless, to capture the difference between beavers building dams and urban sprawl, we distinguished between humans and the rest of nature (which is what "nature" and "environment" have meant since Chapter 2). Some such distinction seems to be necessary in order to make the construction of suburbs ethically salient in a way that the building of dams by beavers is not. We want to hold humans morally responsible for urban sprawl in a way we do not want to hold beavers responsible for their dams, even if those dams have severe effects on their surroundings including, for instance, the destruction of habitats of other, perhaps critically endangered, species.

Yet it is this distinction between humanity and nature, though construed as having more metaphysical weight, that is used by wilderness advocates to underwrite a sharp distinction between natural environments and those that are even partly products of human action (Chapter 2). In the same vein, critics of habitat reconstruction (including ecological restoration) often deny that anthropogenically modified habitats have any natural value (Chapter 6). Does this mean that we have to accept these concerns as legitimate? Not necessarily. What we need is a more nuanced understanding of the ways in which humanity is a part of nature, and the ways in which it is different from the rest of nature. Recognizing that you are part of your family does not prevent us from also thinking of you as distinct from the rest of your family. And it certainly does not prevent you from caring about your family. The same applies to nature.

Notes

1. For the National Center for Ecological Analysis and Synthesis working group's analysis of intrinsic value arguments see Maguire and Justus (2008).
2. See Callicott (2006), which is strangely ignored by Maguire and Justus (2008).
3. For a more abstract version of what appears to a be a similar argument to the one being made in the text (or is at least consistent with it), see McShane (2007).
4. See Janzen (1986), p. 306.

Glossary

Algorithm	A mechanical step-by-step procedure to carry out a task, typically implemented as a computer program.
Anthropocentrism	In environmental ethics, the assumption that all value ultimately derives from considerations of the rights, interests, *etc.*, of humans.
Biocentrism	In environmental ethics, the assumption that all value ultimately derives from considerations of both human rights, interests, *etc.*, and what is of benefit to other living entities. (There are many other definitions, but this is the one used in the text.)
Biota	Any biological entity.
Biotic community	See Community.
Community	In ecology, a set of species that are geographically located in the same region and interact with each other.
Complementarity	In systematic conservation planning, the number of new species or other biodiversity surrogate that an area

would bring to an existing set of prioritized areas.

Conservation area network   A set of areas to be managed for the conservation of biodiversity.

Constituent   In systematic conservation planning, any component of biodiversity deemed worthy of conservation.

Ecocentrism   In environmental ethics, the assumption that all value ultimately derives from considerations of humans and all entities that are not primarily of anthropogenic origin. (There are many other definitions, but this is the one used in the text.)

Ecological community   See Community.

Ecosystem   An ecological community and its biophysical surroundings.

Endemic/endemicity   A species or other taxon that is geographically limited in its distribution.

Surrogate   In systematic conservation planning, any feature that can be used to represent or measure biodiversity constituents during a planning exercise.

Taxon/taxa   Any named (taxonomic) group in the hierarchical classification of organisms; for example, species, genus, family, order, class, phylum.

References

Aaltola, E. 2009. "Animal Ethics." In Callicott, J. B. and Frodeman, R. Eds. *Encyclopedia of Environmental Ethics and Philosophy*. Vol. 1 Farmington Hills, MI: Thomson Gale, pp. 42–53.

Agarwal, A. 1992. "Sociological and Political Constraints to Biodiversity Conservation." In Sandlund, O. T., Hinder, K., and Brown, A. H. D. Eds. *Conservation of Biodiversity for Sustainable Development*. Oslo: Scandinavian University Press, pp. 293–302.

Arrow, K. J. 1950. "A Difficulty in the Concept of Social Welfare. " *Journal of Political Economy* **58**: 328–346.

Arrow, K. J. 1963. *Social Choice and Individual Values*. 2nd Ed. New Haven, CT: Yale University Press.

Arrow, K. J. and Raynaud, H. 1986. *Social Choice and Multicriterion Decision-making*. Cambridge, MA: MIT Press.

Ballentine, R. K. and Guarraia, L. J. Eds. 1977. *The Integrity of Water: A Symposium*. Washington, DC: US Environmental Protection Agency Office of Water and Hazardous Materials.

Barlow, M. 2007. *Blue Covenant: The Global Water Crisis and the Coming Battle for the Right to Water*. New York: New Press.

Bindra, P. S. 2008. "Bharatpur – Hope and Birds Return." *Sanctuary Asia* **28** (6): 60–61.

Blaikie, P. M. 1985. *The Political Economy of Soil Erosion in Developing Countries*. New York: Wiley.

Bookchin, M. 1995. *The Philosophy of Social Ecology: Essays on Dialectical Naturalism*. Montréal, QC: Black Rose Books.

Boyce, M. S. 1992. "Population Viability Analysis." *Annual Review of Ecology and Systematics* **23**: 481–497.

Environmental Philosophy: From Theory to Practice, First Edition. Sahotra Sarkar.
© 2012 John Wiley & Sons Inc. Published 2012 by John Wiley & Sons Inc.

Cairns Jr., J. 1977. "Quantification of Biological Integrity." In Ballentine, R. K.and Guarraia, L. J. Eds. *The Integrity of Water*. Washington, DC: US Environmental Protection Agency Office of Water and Hazardous Materials, pp. 171–187.

Callicott, J. B. 1980. "Animal Liberation: A Triangular Affair." *Environmental Ethics* **2**: 331–338.

Callicott, J. B. 1986. "On the Intrinsic Value of Nonhuman Species." In Norton, B. G. Ed. *The Preservation of Species: The Value of Biological Diversity*. Princeton, NJ: Princeton University Press, pp. 138–172.

Callicott, J. B. 1989. *In Defense of the Land Ethic: Essays in Environmental Philosophy*. Albany, NY: State University of New York Press.

Callicott, J. B. 2002. "Choosing Appropriate Temporal and Spatial Scales for Ecological Restoration." *Journal of Biosciences* **27** (S2): 409–420.

Callicott, J. B. 2006. "Explicit and Implicit Values." In Scott, J. M., Goble, D. D., and Davis, F. W. Eds. *The Endangered Species Act at Thirty. Vol. 2. Conserving Biodiversity in Human-Dominated Landscapes*. Washington, DC: Island Press, pp. 36–48.

Callicott, J. B. and Mumford, K. 1997. "Ecological Sustainability as a Conservation Concept." *Conservation Biology* **11**: 32–40.

Callicott, J. B. and Nelson, M. P. Eds. 1998. *The Great New Wilderness Debate*. Athens, GA: University of Georgia Press.

Callicott, J. B. and Nelson, M. P. Eds. 2008. *The Wilderness Debate Rages On: Continuing the Great New Wilderness Debate*. Athens, GA: University of Georgia Press.

Caufield, C. 1984. *In the Rainforest: Report from a Strange, Beautiful, Imperiled World*. Chicago, IL: University of Chicago Press.

Ciarleglio, M., Barnes, J. W., and Sarkar, S. 2009. "ConsNet: New Software for the Selection of Conservation Area Networks with Spatial and Multi-Criteria Analyses." *Ecography* **32**: 205–209.

Clarke, A. L. 2001. "The Sierra Club and Immigration Policy: A Critique." *Politics and Life Sciences* **20**: 29–38.

[COMEST] World Commission on the Ethics of Science and Technology. 2005. "The Precautionary Principle." Report. Paris: UNESCO.

Conservation International. 2010. "Optimizing Conservation and Production – A Collaboration between Conservation and Business." Report. Jakarta: Conservation International – Indonesia.

Costanza, R., d'Arge, R., de Groot, R., Farber, S., Grasso, M., Hannon, B., Limburg, K., Naeem, S., O'Neill, R. V., Paruelo, J., Raskin, R. G., Sutton,

P., and van den Belt, M. 1997. "The Value of the World's Ecosystem Services and Natural Capital." *Nature* **387**: 253–260.

Council on Environmental Quality and US Department of State 1981. *The Global 2000 Report to the President*. Charlottesville, VA: Blue Angel.

Crist, E. 2009. "Social Ecology." In Callicott, J. B. and Frodeman, R. Eds. *Encyclopedia of Environmental Ethics and Philosophy*. Vol. **2** Farmington Hills, MI: Thomson Gale, pp. 253–258.

Cronon, W. 1996. "The Trouble with Wilderness; or, Getting Back to the Wrong Nature." In Cronon, W. Ed. *Uncommon Ground: Rethinking the Human Place in Nature*. New York: W. W. Norton, pp. 69–90.

Cypher, J. and Higgs, E. 1997. "Colonizing the Imagination: Disney's Wilderness Lodge." *Capitalism, Nature, Socialism* **8**: 107–130.

Daly, H. E. and Cobb, J. B. 1989. *For the Common Good: Redirecting the Economy Toward Community, the Environment, and a Sustainable Future*. Boston, MA: Beacon Press.

d'Amasio, R. 1994. *Descartes' Error: Emotion, Reason, and the Human Brain*. New York: Putnam.

Darwin, C. 1871. *The Descent of Man, and Selection in Relation to Sex*. London: John Murray.

Dasmann, R. F. 1959. *Environmental Conservation*. New York: John Wiley & Sons.

Davion, V. 2001. "Ecofeminism." In Jamieson, D. Ed. *A Companion to Environmental Philosophy*. Malden, MA: Blackwell, pp. 233–247.

Donlan, C. J., Berger, J., Bock, J. H., Burney, D. A., Estes, J. A., Foreman, D., Martin, P. S., Roemer, G. W., Smith, F. A., Soulé, M. E., and Greene, H.W. 2005. "Pleistocene Rewilding: An Optimistic Agenda for Twenty-First Century Conservation." *American Naturalist* **168**: 660–681.

Dowie, M. 2009. *Conservation Refugees*. Cambridge, MA: MIT Press.

Drengson, A. and Inoue, Y. Eds. 1995. *The Deep Ecology Movement: An Introductory Anthology*. Berkeley, CA: North Atlantic Books.

Dyer, J. and Sarin, R. 1979. Measurable Multiattribute Value Functions. *Operations Research* **27**: 810–822.

Edgerton, F. N. 1973. "Changing Concepts of Balance of Nature." *Quarterly Review of Biology* **48**: 322–350.

Ehrenfeld, D. W. 1976. "The Conservation of Non-Resources." *American Scientist* **64**: 648–656.

Elliot, R. 1997. *Faking Nature: The Ethics of Environmental Restoration*. London: Routledge.

Elliott, R. 2001. "Normative Ethics." In Jamieson, D. Ed. *A Companion to Environmental Philosophy*. Oxford, UK: Blackwell, pp. 175–191.

Elton, C. S. 1958. *The Ecology of Invasions by Animals and Plants*. London: Methuen.

Ferry, L. 1995. *The New Ecological Order*. Chicago, IL: University of Chicago Press.

Figueroa, R. 2009. "Environmental Justice." In Callicott, J. B. and Frodeman, R. Eds. *Encyclopedia of Environmental Ethics and Philosophy*. Vol. 1 Farmington Hills, MI: Thomson Gale, pp. 341–348.

Figueroa, R. and Mills, C. 2001. "Environmental Justice." In Jamieson, D. Ed. *A Companion to Environmental Philosophy*. Malden, MA: Blackwell, pp. 426–436.

Folke, C., Carpenter, S., Walker, B., Scheffer, M., Elmqvist, T., Gunderson, L., and Holling, C. S. 2004. "Regime Shifts, Resilience, and Biodiversity in Ecosystem Management." *Annual Review of Ecology, Evolution, and Systematics* **35**: 557–581.

Foreman, D. 1991. "Second Thoughts of an Eco-Warrior." In Chase, S. Ed. *Defending the Earth: A Dialogue Between Murray Bookchin and Dave Foreman*. Boston, MA: South End Press, pp. 107–119.

Frank, D. M. and Sarkar, S. 2010. "Group Decisions in Biodiversity Conservation: Implications from Game Theory." *PLoS ONE* **5** (5): e10688. doi: 10.1371/journal.pone.0010688.

Franke, R. and Chasin, B. H. 1981. "Peasants, Peanuts, Profits and Pastoralists." *Ecologist* **11**: 156–168.

Frankena, W. K. 1939. "The Naturalistic Fallacy." *Mind* **48**: 464–477.

Garvey, J. 2008. *The Ethics of Climate Change*. London: Continuum.

Gilpin, M. E. and Soulé, M. E. 1986. "Minimum Viable Populations: Processes of Species Extinction." In Soulé, M. E. Ed. *Conservation Biology: The Science of Scarcity and Diversity*. Sunderland, MA: Sinauer, pp. 19–34.

Gosseries, A. and Meyer, L. Eds. 2009. *Intergenerational Justice*. Oxford, UK: Oxford University Press.

Gould, S. J. and Lewontin, R. C. 1979. "The Spandrels of San Marco and the Panglossian Paradigm." *Proceedings of the Royal Society of London B* **205**: 581–598.

Greenberg, J. B. and Park, T. K. 1994. "Political Ecology." *Journal of Political Ecology* **1**: 1–12.

References

Grimm, V. and Wissel, C. 1997. "Babel, or the Ecological Stability Discussions: An Inventory and Analysis of Terminology and a Guide for Avoiding Confusions." *Oecologia* **109**: 323–334.

Guangwei, C. Ed. 2002. *Biodiversity in the Eastern Himalayas: Conservation through Dialogue*. Kathmandu: International Centre for Integrated Mountain Development (ICIMOD).

Guha, R. 1989a. "Radical American Environmentalism and Wilderness Preservation: A Third World Critique." *Environmental Ethics* **11**: 71–83.

Guha, R. 1989b. *The Unquiet Woods: Ecological Change and Peasant Resistance in the Himalaya*. New Delhi: Oxford University Press.

Guha, R. Ed. 1994. *Social Ecology*. Delhi: Oxford University Press.

Hall, M. 2005. *Earth Repair: A Transatlantic History of Environmental Restoration*. Charlottesville, VA: University of Virginia Press.

Higgs, E. 2003. *Nature by Design: People, Natural Processes, and Ecological Restoration*. Cambridge, MA: MIT Press.

Hoegh-Guldberg, O., Hughes, L., McIntyre, S., Lindenmayer, D. B., Parmesan, C., Possingham, H. P., and Thomas, C. D. 2008. "Assisted Colonization and Rapid Climate Change." *Science* **321**: 345–346.

Holland, A. 2001. "Sustainability." In Jamieson, D. Ed. *A Companion to Environmental Philosophy*. Malden, MA: Blackwell, pp. 390–401.

Holling, C. S. 1973. "Resilience and Stability of Ecological Systems." *Annual Review of Ecology and Systematics* **4**: 1–23.

Holling, C. S. Ed. 1978. *Adaptive Environmental Assessment and Management*. Chichester, UK: Wiley.

Hume, D. 1972 [1737] *A Treatise on Human Nature*. London: Fontana.

Intergovernmental Panel on Climate Change. 2000. *Summary For Policymakers: Emissions Scenarios*. Geneva, Switzerland: Intergovernmental Panel on Climate Change.

Jamieson, D. 2008. *Ethics and the Environment*. Cambridge, UK: Cambridge University Press.

Jamieson, D. 2009. "Global Climate Change." In Callicott, J. B. and Frodeman, R. Eds. *Encyclopedia of Environmental Ethics and Philosophy*. Vol. **1** Farmington Hills, MI: Thomson Gale, pp. 458–463.

Janzen, D. 1986. "The Future of Tropical Ecology." *Annual Review of Ecology and Systematics* **17**: 305–324.

Justus, J. and Sarkar, S. 2002. "The Principle of Complementarity in the Design of Reserve Networks to Conserve Biodiversity: A Preliminary History." *Journal of Biosciences* **27** (S2): 421–443.

Karr, J. R. and Dudley, D. R. 1981. "Ecological Perspective on Water Quality Goals." *Environmental Management* **5**: 55–68.

Keeney, R. L. and Raiffa, H. 1993. *Decisions with Multiple Objectives: Preferences and Value Tradeoffs.* Cambridge, UK: Cambridge University Press.

Keller, D. R. 2009. "Deep Ecology." In Callicott, J. B. and Frodeman, R. Eds. *Encyclopedia of Environmental Ethics and Philosophy.* Vol. **1** Farmington Hills, MI: Thomson Gale, pp. 206–211.

Kingsland, S. E. 2002. "Designing Nature Reserves: Adapting Ecology to Real-World Problems." *Endeavour* **26**: 9–14.

Konikow, L. F. and Kendy, E. 2005. "Groundwater Depletion: A Global Problem." *Hydrogeological Journal* **13**: 317–320.

Latour, B. 2004. *Politics of Nature: How to Bring Sciences into Democracy.* Cambridge, MA: Harvard University Press.

Lee, M. F. 1995. *Earth First! Environmental Apocalypse.* Syracuse, NY: Syracuse University Press.

Leopold, A. 1949. *A Sand County Almanac.* New York: Oxford University Press.

Levi, I. 1986. *Hard Choices.* Cambridge, UK: Cambridge University Press.

Levins, R. 1966. "The Strategy of Model Building in Population Biology." *American Scientist* **54**: 421–431.

Levins, R. 1993. "A Response to Orzack and Sober: Formal Analysis and the Fluidity of Science." *Quarterly Review of Biology* **68**: 547–555.

Lewontin, R. C., Rose, S., and Kamin, L. J. 1984. *Not in Our Genes: Biology, Ideology, and Human Nature.* Cambridge, MA: Harvard University Press.

Loomis, J. B. and White, D. S. 1996. "Economic benefits of Rare and Endangered Species: Summary and Meta-analysis." *Ecological Economics* **18**: 197–206.

Lubchenco, J., Olson, A. M., Brubaker, L. B., Carpenter, S. R., Holland, M. M., Hubbell, S. P., Levin, S. A., MacMahon, J. A., Matson, P. A., Melillo, J. M., Mooney, H. A., Peterson, C. H., Pulliam, H. R., Real, L. A., Regal, P. J., and Risser, P. G. 1991. "The Sustainable Biosphere Initiative: An Ecological Research Agenda." *Ecology* **72**: 371–412.

MacArthur, R. A. 1955. "Fluctuations of Animal Populations and a Measure of Community Stability." *Ecology* **36**: 533–536.

MacKay, A. F. 1980. *Arrow's Theorem: The Paradox of Social Choice.* New Haven, CT: Yale University Press.

References

MacLaurin, J. and Sterelny, K. 2008. *What is Biodiversity?* Chicago, IL: University of Chicago Press.

Maffi, L. Ed. 2001. *On Biocultural Diversity: Linking Language, Knowledge, and the Environment.* Washington, DC: Smithsonian Institution Press.

Maguire, L. and Justus, J. 2008. "Why Intrinsic Value is a Poor Basis for Conservation Decisions." *BioScience* **58**: 910–911.

Magurran, A. E. 1988. *Ecological Diversity and its Measurement.* Princeton, NJ: Princeton University Press.

Magurran, A. E. 2003. *Measuring Biological Diversity.* Oxford, UK: Blackwell.

Malhotra, K. C., Gokhale, Y., Chatterjee, S., and Srivastava. S. 2007. *Sacred Groves in India: An Overview.* New Delhi: Aryan Books International.

Mann, C. C. and Plummer, M. L. 1995. *Noah's Choice: The Future of Endangered Species.* New York: A. A. Knopf.

Margules, C. R. and Pressey, R. L. 2000. "Systematic Conservation Planning." *Nature* **405**: 245–253.

Margules, C. R. and Sarkar, S. 2007. *Systematic Conservation Planning.* Cambridge, UK: Cambridge University Press.

Martinez-Alier, J. 2002. *The Environmentalism of the Poor: A Study of Ecological Conflicts and Valuation.* Cheltenham, UK: Edward Elgar.

Martinich, A. 2005. *Hobbes.* London: Routledge.

May, R. M. 1973. *Stability and Complexity in Model Ecosystems.* Princeton, NJ: Princeton University Press.

McKibben, B. 1989. *The End of Nature: Humanity, Climate Change and the Natural World.* New York: Random House.

McShane, K. 2007. "Why Environmental Ethics Shouldn't Give Up on Intrinsic Value." *Environmental Ethics* **29**: 43–61.

Meadows, D. H., Meadows, D. L., Randers, J., and Behrens, W. W. 1972. *The Limits to Growth.* New York: Universe.

Meehl, G. A., Stocker, T. F., Collins, W. D., Friedlingstein, P., Gaye, A. T., Gregory, J. M., Kitoh, A., Knutti, R., Murphy, J. M., Noda, A., Raper, S. C. B., Watterson, I. G., Weaver, A. J., and Zhao, Z.-C. 2007. "Global Climate Projections." In Solomon, S., Qin, D., Manning, M., Chen, Z., Marquis, M., Averyt, K. B., Tignor, M., and Miller, H. L. Eds. *Climate Change 2007: The Physical Science Basis. Contribution of Working Group I to the Fourth Assessment Report of the Intergovernmental Panel on Climate Change.* Cambridge, UK: Cambridge University Press, pp. 747–845.

References

Merchant, C. 1983. *The Death of Nature: Women, Ecology, and the Scientific Revolution*. New York: Harper & Row.

Minteer, B. A. and Collins, J. P. 2008. "From Environmental to Ecological Ethics: Toward a Practical Ethics for Ecologists and Conservationists." *Science and Engineering Ethics* **14**: 483–501.

Moffett, A., Dyer, J. S., and Sarkar, S. 2006. "Integrating Biodiversity Representation with Multiple Criteria in North-Central Namibia Using Non-Dominated Alternatives and a Modified Analytic Hierarchy Process." *Biological Conservation* **129**: 181–191.

Moffett, A. and Sarkar, S. 2006. "Incorporating Multiple Criteria into the Design of Conservation Area Networks: A Minireview with Recommendations." *Diversity and Distributions* **12**: 125–137.

Moilanen, A., Possingham, H., and Wilson, K. Eds. 2009. *Spatial Conservation Prioritization: Quantitative Methods and Computational Tools*. Oxford, UK: Oxford University Press.

Moore, G. E. 1903. *Principia Ethica*. Cambridge, UK: Cambridge University Press.

Morton, A. 1991. *Disasters and Dilemmas: Strategies for Real-life Decision Making*. Oxford, UK: Basil Blackwell.

Næss, A. 1986. "Intrinsic Value: Will the Defenders of Nature Please Rise?" In Soulé, M. E. Ed. *Conservation Biology: The Science of Scarcity and Diversity*. Sunderland, MA: Sinauer, pp. 504–515.

Næss, A. 1989. *Ecology, Community and Lifestyle: Outline of an Ecosophy*. Cambridge, UK: Cambridge University Press.

Næss, A. 1995 [1973] "The Shallow and the Deep, Long-Range Ecology Movement." In Drengson, A. and Inoue, Y. Eds. *The Deep Ecology Movement: An Introductory Anthology*. Berkeley, CA: North Atlantic Books, pp. 3–9.

Næss, A. and Sessions, G. 1995 [1984] "Platform Principles of the Deep Ecology Movement." In Drengson, A. and Inoue, Y. Eds. *The Deep Ecology Movement: An Introductory Anthology*. Berkeley, CA: North Atlantic Books, pp. 49–53.

Nash, R. 1973. *Wilderness and the American Mind*. 2nd ed. New Haven, CT: Yale University Press.

National Research Council. 1992. *Restoration of Aquatic Ecosystems*. Washington, DC: National Academy Press.

National Research Council. 2003. *Science and the Greater Everglades Ecosystem Restoration*. Washington, DC: National Academies Press.

References

Neumann, R. P. 2004. "Moral and Discursive Geographies in the War for Biodiversity in Africa." *Political Geography* **23**: 813–837.

Norton, B. G. 1987. *Why Preserve Natural Variety?* Princeton, NJ: Princeton University Press.

Norton, B. G. 2005. *Sustainability: A Philosophy of Adaptive Ecosystem Management*. Chicago, IL: University of Chicago Press.

Odenbaugh, J. 2003. "Complex Systems, Trade-Offs and Mathematical Modeling: A Response to Sober and Orzack." *Philosophy of Science* **70**: 1496–1507.

Odenbaugh, J. 2005. "Ecology." In Sarkar, S. and Pfeifer, J. Eds. *The Philosophy of Science: An Encyclopedia*. New York: Routledge, pp. 215–224.

Okonta, I. and Douglas, O. 2003. *Where Vultures Feast: Shell, Human Rights, and Oil*. London: Verso.

Orzack, S. H. and Sober, E. 1993. "A Critical Assessment of Levins's *The Strategy of Model Building in Population Biology* (1966)." *Quarterly Review of Biology* **68**: 533–546.

Parfit, D. 1984. *Reasons and Persons*. Oxford, UK: Clarendon Press.

Patil, G. P. and Taillie, C. 1982. "Diversity as a Concept and its Measurement." *Journal of the American Statistical Association* **77**: 548–561.

Pearce, D. W., Hamilton, K., and Atkinson, G. 1996. "Measuring Sustainable Development: Progress on Indicators." *Environment and Development Economics* **1**: 85–101.

Peterson, M. 2006. "The Precautionary Principle is Incoherent." *Risk Analysis* **26**: 595–601.

Pimentel, D. 1961. "Species Diversity and Insect Population Outbreaks." *Annals of the Entomological Society of America* **54**: 76–86.

Pimm, S. L. 1991. *The Balance of Nature? Ecological Issues in the Conservation of Species and Communities*. Chicago, IL: University of Chicago Press.

Plumwood, V. 1993. *Feminism and the Mystery of Nature*. London: Routledge.

Pyne, S. J. 1982. *Fire in America: A Cultural History of Wildland and Rural Fire*. Princeton, NJ: Princeton University Press.

Rangan, H. 2000. *Of Myths and Movements: Rewriting Chipko into Himalayan History*. London: Verso.

Resnik, D. B. 2003. "Is the Precautionary Principle Unscientific?" *Studies in the History and Philosophy of Biological and Biomedical Sciences* **34**: 329–344.

Resnik, M. D. 1987. *Choices: An Introduction to Decision Theory*. Minneapolis, MN: University of Minnesota Press.

Revkin, A. 1990. *The Burning Season: The Murder of Chico Mendes and the Fight for the Amazon Rain Forest*. Boston, MA: Houghton Mifflin.

Ricciardi, A. and Simberloff, D. B. 2009. "Assisted Colonization is Not a Viable Conservation Strategy." *Trends in Ecology and Evolution* **24**: 248–253.

Richardson, D. M., Hellmann, J. J., McLachlan, J. S., Sax, D. F., Schwartz, M. W., Gonzalez, P., Brennan, E. J., Camacho, A., Root, T. L., Sala, O. E., Schneider, S. H., Ashe, D. M., Clark, J. R., Regan, E., Etterson, J. R., Fielder, E. D., Gill, J. L., Minteer, B. A., Polasky, S., Safford, H. D., Thompson, A. R., and Vellend, M. 2009. "Multidimensional Evaluation of Managed Relocation." *Proceedings of the National Academy of Sciences (USA)* **106**: 9721–9724.

Rosenberg, A. 2006. *Darwinian Reductionism: Or, How to Stop Worrying and Love Molecular Biology*. Chicago, IL: University of Chicago Press.

Rubenstein, D. R., Rubenstein, D. I., Sherman, P. W., and Gavin, T. A. 2006. "Pleistocene Park: Does Re-Wilding North America Represent Sound Conservation for the 21st Century?" *Biological Conservation* **132**: 232–238.

Sachse, C. 2007. *Reductionism in the Philosophy of Science*. Frankfurt, Germany: Onto Verlag.

Sandler, R. 2010. "The Value of Species and the Ethical Foundations of Assisted Colonization." *Conservation Biology* **24**: 424–431.

Sandlund, O. T., Hinder, K., and Brown, A. H. D. Eds. 1992. *Conservation of Biodiversity for Sustainable Development*. Oslo: Scandinavian University Press.

Sansom, A. 2008. *Water in Texas*. Austin, TX: University of Texas Press.

Sarakinos, H., Nicholls, A. O., Tubert, A., Aggarwal, A., Margules, C. R., and Sarkar, S. 2001. "Area Prioritization for Biodiversity Conservation in Québec on the Basis of Species Distributions: A Preliminary Analysis." *Biodiversity and Conservation* **10**: 1419–1472.

Sarkar, S. 1998a. *Genetics and Reductionism*. Cambridge, UK: Cambridge University Press.

Sarkar, S. 1998b. "Restoring Wilderness or Reclaiming Forests?" *Terra Nova* **3** (3): 35–52.

Sarkar, S. 1999. "Wilderness Preservation and Biodiversity Conservation – Keeping Divergent Goals Distinct." *BioScience* **49**: 405–412.

Sarkar, S. 2002. "Defining 'Biodiversity'; Assessing Biodiversity." *The Monist* **85**: 131–155.

References

Sarkar, S. 2003. "Conservation Area Networks." *Conservation and Society* **1** (2): v–vii.

Sarkar, S. 2005. *Biodiversity and Environmental Philosophy: An Introduction to the Issues.* Cambridge, UK: Cambridge University Press.

Sarkar, S. 2007a. *Doubting Darwin? Creationist Designs on Evolution.* Oxford, UK: Blackwell.

Sarkar, S. 2007b. "From Ecological Diversity to Biodiversity." In Hull, D. L. and Ruse, M. Eds. *The Cambridge Companion to the Philosophy of Biology.* Cambridge, UK: Cambridge University Press, pp. 388–409.

Sarkar, S. 2008. "Norms and the Conservation of Biodiversity." *Resonance* **13**: 627–637.

Sarkar, S. 2010. "Diversity: A Philosophical Perspective." *Diversity,* **2**: 127–141.

Sarkar, S. 2011. "Habitat Reconstruction: Beyond Historical Fidelity." In Brown, B., de Laplante, K., and Peacock, K. Eds. *Handbook of the Philosophy of Ecology.* New York: Elsevier, pp. 327–361.

Sarkar, S. and Illoldi-Rangel, P. 2010. "Systematic Conservation Planning: An Updated Protocol." *Natureza & Conservação* **8**: 19–26.

Sarkar, S. and Margules, C. R. 2002. "Operationalizing Biodiversity for Conservation Planning." *Journal of Biosciences* **27** (S2): 299–308.

Sarkar, S. and Montoya, M. 2010. "Beyond Parks and Reserves: The Ethics and Politics of Conservation with a Case Study from Peru." *Biological Conservation,* **144**: 979–988.

Sarkar, S., Pappas, C., Garson, J., Aggarwal, A., and Cameron, S. 2004. "Place Prioritization for Biodiversity Conservation using Probabilistic Surrogate Distribution Data." *Diversity and Distributions* **10**: 125–133.

Sarkar, S., Pressey, R. L., Faith, D. P., Margules, C. R., Fuller, T., Stoms, D. M., Moffett, A., Wilson, K., Williams, K. J., Williams, P. H., and Andelman, S. 2006. "Biodiversity Conservation Planning Tools: Present Status and Challenges for the Future." *Annual Review of Environment and Resources* **31**: 123–159.

Schweitzer, A. 1976. *Civilization and Ethics.* Englewood Cliffs, NJ: Prentice-Hall.

Shiva, V. 1990. "Development as a New Project of Western Patriarchy." In Diamond, I. and Ornstein, G. F. Eds. *Reweaving the World: The Emergence of Ecofeminism.* San Francisco, CA: Sierra Club Books, pp. 189–200.

Singer, P. 1975. *Animal Liberation.* New York: New York Review.

Singer, P. 2001. "Animals." In Jamieson, D. Ed. *A Companion to Environmental Philosophy*. Oxford, UK: Blackwell, pp. 416–415.

Sober, E. 1986. "Philosophical Problems for Environmentalism." In Norton, B. G. Ed. *The Preservation of Species*. Princeton, NJ: Princeton University Press, pp. 173–194.

Solow, R. M. 1993. "Sustainability: An Economist's Perspective." In Dorfman, R. and Dorfman, N. S. Eds. *Economics of the Environment*. New York: W. W. Norton, pp. 179–187.

Soulé, M. E. 1985. "What is Conservation Biology?" *BioScience* **35**: 727–734.

Soulé, M. E. 1987. "History of the Society for Conservation Biology: How and Why We Got Here." *Conservation Biology* **1**: 4–5.

Soulé, M. E. and Terborgh, J. Eds. 1999. *Continental Conservation: Scientific Foundations of Regional Reserve Networks*. Washington DC: Island Press.

Spence, M. D. 2000. *Dispossessing the Wilderness: Indian Removal and the Making of the National Parks*. New York: Oxford University Press.

Stirling, A. 2007. "Risk, Precaution and Science: Towards a More Constructive Policy Debate." *European Molecular Biology Organization Reports* **8**: 309–315.

Stone, C. D. 1974. *Should Trees Have Standing? Toward Legal Rights for Natural Objects*. Los Altos, CA: William Kauffman.

Stone, C. D. 1985. "*Should Trees Have Standing?* Revisited: How Far Will Law and Morals Reach? A Pluralist Perspective." *Southern California Law Review* **59**: 1–156.

Takacs, D. 1996. *The Idea of Biodiversity: Philosophies of Paradise*. Baltimore, MD: Johns Hopkins Press.

Taylor, P. W. 1986. *Respect for Nature: A Theory of Environmental Ethics*. Princeton, NJ: Princeton University Press.

Thacker, C. 1979. *The History of Gardens*. Berkeley, CA: University of California Press.

[UN] United Nations. 1992. *Agenda 21: The UN Programme of Action from Rio*. New York: United Nations.

United Church of Christ Commission for Racial Justice. 1987. *Toxic Wastes and Race in the United States: A National Report on the Racial and Socio-Economic Characteristics of Communities with Hazardous Waste Sites*. New York: Public Data Access, Inc.

United States House of, Representatives. 1993. *Environmental Justice: Hearings before the Subcommittee on Civil and Constitutional Rights,*

Committee on Judiciary, 103rd Congress, 1st Session. Washington, DC: US Government Printing Office.

van Fraassen, B. 1980. *The Scientific Image*. New York: Oxford University Press.

Vane-Wright, R. I., Humphries, C. J., and Williams, P. H. 1991. "What to Protect? Systematics and the Agony of Choice." *Biological Conservation* **55**: 235–254.

Vijayan, V. S. 1987. *Keoladeo National Park Ecology Study*. Bombay, India: Bombay Natural History Society.

von Neumann, J. and Morgenstern, O. 1944. *The Theory of Games and Economic Behavior*. Princeton, NJ: Princeton University Press.

Walker, B., Holling, C. S., Carpenter, S. R., and Kinzig, A. 2004. "Resilience, Adaptability and Transformability in Social–Ecological Systems." *Ecology and Society* **9** (2): 5.

Walker, B. and Salt, D. 2006. *Resilience Thinking*. Washington, DC: Island Press.

Warren, K. J. 2009. "Ecological Feminism." In Callicott, J. B. and Frodeman, R. Eds. *Encyclopedia of Environmental Ethics and Philosophy*. Vol. **1** Farmington Hills, MI: Thomson Gale, pp. 228–236.

Weismann, A. 1889. *Essays Upon Heredity and Kindred Subjects*. Oxford, UK: Clarendon Press.

Welch, L. L. 1994. "Crowd Blasts Species Act at Meeting: Federal Laws Violate Constitution, Speakers in Georgetown Say." *Austin-American Statesman*, September 22, B1.

Wenz, P. S. 1988. *Environmental Justice*. Albany, NY: State University of New York Press.

White, L. 1967. "The Historical Roots of Our Ecological Crisis." *Science* **155**: 1203–1207.

Whittaker, R. H. 1960. "Vegetation of the Siskiyou Mountains, Oregon and California." *Ecological Monographs* **30**: 279–338.

Williams, R. 1980. *Problems in Materialism and Culture*. London: Verso.

Wilson, J. 1999. *Biological Individuality: The Identity and Persistence of Living Entities*. Cambridge, UK: Cambridge University Press.

Wimsatt, W. C. 1980. "Robustness, Reliability, and Overdetermination." In Brewer, M. and Collins, B. Eds. *Scientific Inquiry and the Social Sciences*. San Francisco, CA: Jossey-Bass, pp. 124–163.

Woods, M. 2001. "Wilderness." In Jamieson, D. Ed. *A Companion to Environmental Philosophy*. Oxford, UK: Blackwell, pp. 349–361.

Woods, P. M. 2000. *Biodiversity and Democracy: Rethinking Society and Nature.* Vancouver, BC: University of British Columbia Press.

[WCED] World Commission on Environment and Development. 1987. *Our Common Future.* Oxford, UK: Oxford University Press.

Wynne, B. 1994. "Scientific Knowledge and the Global Environment." In Redclift, M. and Benton, T. Eds. *Social Theory and the Global Environment.* London: Routledge, pp. 169–189.

Index

Environmental Philosophy: From Theory to Practice, First Edition. Sahotra Sarkar.
© 2012 John Wiley & Sons Inc. Published 2012 by John Wiley & Sons Inc.